After graduating from Bristol University in 1967 Elwyn Thomas began a career as a journalist. He set up a publishing group in Greater Manchester in 1979 which he later sold to the *Guardian* and the *Manchester Evening News*. Wanting a change of career he moved into management consultancy, where he specializes in team building and strategic planning. He has also written several articles on these topics for training journals. Elwyn Thomas is married with two children.

Graduating from London University with a Ph.D. in Physical Chemistry, Mike Woods worked with British Coal for ten years as a scientist and later commissioning engineer before joining Unilever. Moving steadily from engineering he became an internal consultant specializing in the 'human issues' of change and finally headed the Unilever UK's middle management training unit. He joined Bradford University Management Centre as a Course Director in 1979 and has been associated with developing and running courses for a range of organizations. He is the author of several books and articles including *The New Manager* and *Working Alone*. He lives in Yorkshire and is happily married with a grown-up family.

The authors currently run a training company based in Bradford.

ELWYN THOMAS AND MIKE WOODS

———

THE MANAGER'S CASEBOOK

A UNIQUE NEW COURSE BRIDGING
THE DIVIDE BETWEEN
MANAGEMENT THEORY AND
REAL PEOPLE DOING REAL JOBS

PENGUIN BOOKS

PENGUIN BOOKS

Published by the Penguin Group
Penguin Books Ltd, 27 Wrights Lane, London W8 5TZ, England
Penguin Books USA Inc., 375 Hudson Street, New York, New York 10014, USA
Penguin Books Australia Ltd, Ringwood, Victoria, Australia
Penguin Books Canada Ltd, 10 Alcorn Avenue, Toronto, Ontario, Canada M4V 3B2
Penguin Books (NZ) Ltd, 182–190 Wairau Road, Auckland 10, New Zealand

Penguin Books Ltd, Registered Offices: Harmondsworth, Middlesex, England

First published by Michael Joseph 1992
Published in Penguin Books 1994
1 3 5 7 9 10 8 6 4 2

CONTENTS

THE INDIVIDUAL

Case Studies

COMMUNICATING WELL

LEADERSHIP

THE TEAM

THE CREATIVE MANAGER

C H A N G E

P O S T S C R I P T

INTRODUCTIONS

> "There are three types of companies. Those who make things happen. Those who watch things happen. Those who wonder what happened."
>
> Mike Woods, 1990

Vulcan Computing falls into the last category. The firm was founded by Duncan Johnson in the mid 1970s. It did well in the early 1980s, but now it has lost its way.

Vulcan have been squeezed by spiralling costs and increased foreign competition. Their rivals found that the only way forward was to import their parts and concentrate on the assembly and distribution of computers.

When the company's bank pointed this out, Duncan stubbornly resisted the advice. Within months, it was too late. He had to bow to the inevitable: forced resignation. Soon after, Stuart Blyth was called in to try and rescue the business.

STUART BLYTH, managing director

Career profile
Stuart Blyth took a degree in economics and began his career with an international computer group. He rapidly moved up the ladder, eventually becoming the youngest area manager at 28. He then went on sensationally to revive the fortunes of three ailing companies within the group.

Ambitious, when he was headhunted for the post of managing director at Vulcan he realized this was just the challenge he needed. His immediate task is to restructure Vulcan, to redefine its object-ives and to implement a new marketing strategy.

Personal profile
Stuart is 38 years old, happily married with two children. Unfortunately, he has not been able to sell his house since joining Vulcan, which means he only sees his family at weekends. He enjoys golf and squash, when he can find the time.

Here is the management team which Stuart has inherited:

CAMPBELL RITCHIE, production director

Career profile
Loyal and hardworking, he has been with the company 13 years. He tends to drive his staff too hard, but they respect him and he really cares about how they regard him. A strong leader, with an old-fashioned sense of values, he is wary about the new strategy Stuart seems to be imposing on the company. He has promised his staff there will be no redundancies. They believe him.

Personal profile
Aged 45 years, he and his wife have bought a small antiques shop with the proceeds of a legacy. Stuart Blyth is aware that Campbell is making his own contingency plans and suspects that his commitment to Vulcan is not as great as it used to be.

BETTY JONES, marketing director

Career profile
Betty recently returned to Vulcan after a messy divorce. She is widely regarded as a single-minded, somewhat calculating manager who is great fun to work with when things are going well. But under pressure she becomes aggressive

and rebellious. Her management style is to play things by ear and to disregard well-prepared plans which her staff have spent considerable time devising. None the less, she has an excellent network of contacts and can get things done.

Personal profile
Betty is enjoying her new-found freedom and is nervous of committing herself to a new long-term relationship. She is finding the pace of her social life rather hectic, and is beginning to slow down.

*H*ELEN DAVIES, personnel manager

Career profile
She has all the necessary qualifications for the job and is extremely conscientious. She has introduced modern methods of selection and assessment into the company, overcoming considerable opposition in the process, especially from Campbell. Despite this, she is not a particularly good manager and is regarded as ineffective by her colleagues.

Personal profile
Aged 34, married with two children, Helen is content, and somewhat smug. She strongly disapproves of Betty's lifestyle, but dislikes confrontation and is inclined to bite her tongue.

*A*LAN DAWSON, financial director

Career profile
Alan has been with the company since its formation. He is proud of his, and the company's achievements, always reminding everyone how hard it was "when Duncan Johnson and I first

started the company". He qualified by going to night school and is acknowledged as being a sound and pragmatic manager. He is fussy, unwilling to take risks, and sceptical of the new regime at Vulcan.

Personal profile
Aged 59, he is looking forward to retirement when he will be able to concentrate more on his beloved garden.

And finally the new member of the team brought in by Stuart:

*M*ATTHEW DAVIES, chief accountant

Career profile
A business school graduate, he worked for a firm of accountants before joining Vulcan Computers. Stuart Blyth has earmarked him to take over from Alan Dawson on the latter's retirement. Much is expected of this comparative youngster.

Personal profile
Aged 28, Matthew lives with his girlfriend in a farmhouse which they are currently restoring.

THE INDIVIDUAL

ADJUSTING TO A NEW JOB — AND NEW PEOPLE

> Truth is a rare and precious commodity.
> We must be sparing in its use
>
> C.P. Scott, The *Spectator* 1982

Matthew has just joined Vulcan Computers as chief accountant and although he is confident of his own abilities, he is nervous.

He has little business experience and no formal management training. His new colleagues are all experienced managers.

He is unsure which of them to trust. He is by nature quite sociable but realizes he will have to be rather cautious at first with his new colleagues. He has no idea at this stage who will become a friend and who might be a threat.

Like most people in a new job he is conscious that:

1. There are some things about himself which he does not want anybody to find out.
2. There are other aspects which he knows must be revealed, but only to a limited circle of trusted confidants.
3. He has some characteristics which he can allow to become public knowledge.

In this section, we show how Matthew made his choices about what, in each category, he should reveal. This is something any new manager must consider seriously. If you were Matthew, would you make the same choices as him? If not, why not?

Skeleton in the cupboard
Matthew never graduated from university. He had a nervous breakdown in the final year. Stuart Blyth knows about this already. Does Matthew need to tell anyone else?

Answer

No. If he has been open and honest with his managing director he cannot be accused of misleading the company as to his suitability for the job. In any case, it is not an important issue, even though Matthew feels sensitive about it. Matthew is good at his job and the lack of an academic qualification is no longer relevant. Nevertheless, Matthew prefers not to tell anyone else about it, and there is simply no need for them to know.

The only short-term danger would be if he fell out of favour with Stuart, who could then use this weak spot as a weapon against him. But then Matthew could say that Stuart had been part of the conspiracy of silence. If Stuart left the company, Matthew would then have to decide if the matter was worth bringing up at all. In, say, five years' time, it is doubtful whether Stuart's replacement would need to know or would even be interested in the fact.

Fear of public speaking
This is something Matthew dreads. Stuart has told him that he will have to speak at major company occasions, and that he will also be expected to talk at leaving ceremonies and other social occasions. Whom does he tell?

Answer

His secretary definitely needs to know. She makes his appointments: Matthew should make sure that she limits his public speaking dates to the minimum.

Matthew could also confide this problem to a few colleagues later on. He might even find that some of them share his phobia. But he needs to choose his confidants. If, for instance, he overhears Betty ridiculing another colleague who "shrivelled up at last night's sales presentation", Matthew would do well to keep quiet.

On the other hand, he might discover that Campbell enjoys the chance to talk to a large audience, and that Campbell would be pleased to take over such duties from Matthew...

3 **Must not drink alcohol**
Matthew suffered from jaundice when he was a child and ought not to drink alcohol. This can be embarrassing at some social occasions when he is expected to drink. Whom does he tell?

Answer

He is likely to mix extensively with his immediate colleagues and they need to be told before the situation arises. If he withheld this information it might be counter-productive. His colleagues who do drink alcohol might take offence and brand him a 'misery'. As time goes on more and more staff are likely to find out about it, so Matthew should decide to let it become public knowledge immediately.

*T*HEORY

The transition from being managed to managing involves major re-adjustment.

We all contain 'different' people and these people can be surprisingly different animals. Campbell, for instance, is one person as Vulcan's production director, one person at home and another at the golf club. All these characteristics are long-established, stable and honed by experience.

Matthew has no such stability. He must create his new management personality from scratch. Moreover, it can only be created by giving things away about himself – this, after all, is the pre-condition of any relationship.

■ The fact that he is unable to drink alcohol is soon well known by everyone at Vulcan. Everyone understands, it ceases to be an issue.
■ Matthew eventually tells Campbell about his public speaking phobia and is surprised to hear that Campbell once suffered from the same problem. "I'll tell you what, Matthew, why don't you go on a two-day speaking course? I can give you the telephone number." Only Stuart Blyth knows about Matthew's failure to finish his university course and the two of them never mention it.

Regard your personality as something like a window. Windows can have:

Clear glass: everyone can see in.

Shutters: opened under certain circumstances.

Blackened glass: anything behind remains hidden.

Managers in new jobs need to exert particularly active control over this window. As time went by and Matthew became more confident, he opened more shutters. For example, he gradually let it be known that he was a big motor-racing fan. So staff were not surprised that Vulcan was part-sponsoring a Formula Two team later that year. Having reached this level of confidence, Matthew could well have considered taking out a long-term 'insurance policy' to protect him from unscrupulous opponents taking advantage of his particular skeleton in the cupboard. Sadly, this is a real possibility when a young executive has had rapid promotion.

Matthew was quite right not to mention his nervous breakdown in his first months at Vulcan, because he could not have been certain whom to trust. After, say, nine months or a year, he should have gained one or two trusted colleagues with whom to share the confidence.

> ■ Spreading the knowledge in this way diffuses the potentially damaging effect of the 'secret' coming to light.

If, for instance, someone outside Vulcan, privy to Matthew's early career, should tell Alan, and Alan, who feels threatened by Matthew (*see case study 2*) deliberately spread the tit-bit around the juniors in the accounts department, serious questions might then be raised about Matthew's fitness to manage, especially if he went through a patch of poor performance. If the breakdown is used against him in this way, Matthew must be able to shrug it off: "Oh that. It's no secret. Ask Betty or Campbell – or Stuart for that matter. They know all about it. They've always felt it's irrelevant."

*E*XERCISE

Write down about 20 points which you think could prevent you from being effective as a manager. Examples could include:

1 I don't really understand accounts.

2 I keep getting into pointless rows.

3 I don't enjoy talking to large groups.

4 I am not a natural diplomat.

As you compile the list, try filling in the adjoining box: dark if it is something you want completely hidden; shaded if you think it best restricted to a limited circulation and not shaded at all if you think it should become common knowledge.

1 ☐   ✍ ....

2 ☐   ✍ ....

3 ☐   ✍ ....

4 ☐   ✍ ....

5 ☐   ✍ ....

Don't evade the decisions. Whatever you hide will probably find you out in the end. The point of the exercise is deciding when you break the news.

Now go through the points again, marking them in the same way, only imagine you are not yet in management. Compare the results: are there differences? What does this tell you?

LOOKING AT PERSONAL STRENGTHS AND WEAKNESSES

> It is as hard to see oneself as to
> look around without turning backwards
> Thoreau

Vulcan's financial director Alan Dawson felt vulnerable. He was 59 years old and simply could not afford to take early retirement. But he knew that he would be lucky to survive in his present post for another full year.

He had lost his closest ally – Duncan Johnson (with whom he had helped found Vulcan) – and he did not know much about Duncan's successor, Stuart Blyth. The whole company was in a state of turmoil and, to make matters worse, he now faced a rival in Matthew Davies, who was being groomed as his successor.

Admittedly, he was not under immediate threat; there was no need to panic, but he realized that he only had limited time in which to act.

His options

> *1* He could analyse his own position without outside help.

> *2* He could ask his wife and friends for guidance.

> *3* He could seek professional advice, either from within the company (Helen in Personnel for instance) or from outside.

Think about these options in the light of your own experience. If you were overlooked for promotion, or did not get enough credit for a job well done, how would you react? Would you strike out in anger, or would you carefully weigh up the situation, as Alan tried to do?

Verdict *1* ▶ **Tackling the problem alone**

This depends on the scale of the problem and the ability of the individual to handle it. Do you need the help of a lawyer to clarify the implications of a contract of employment? Or an insurance broker to discuss your pension plan?

If you have limited experience of management, remember that many people have been in your position before, and that an 'old head' may well provide immediate, useful pointers. Alan, as it happens, had a wealth of experience behind him and he was more than capable of sorting out this problem by himself.

2 ▶ **Consulting spouse and/or friends**

This is not always advisable. They are more than likely to take your side and at best will simply reflect your own views. You sometimes need someone to play devil's advocate. Rely on family and friends for moral support, not for career advice.

3 ▶ **Seeking professional advice**

At first glance this may look like the most sensible option, but it is not necessarily the best one. If Alan had discussed the matter privately with Helen, she would have felt an uncomfortable conflict of interests since she was not only a colleague of Alan's but the personnel manager who helped to recruit Matthew. Anyhow, Alan and Helen had never been particularly close colleagues. People usually ask advice in order to confirm that they are right or that there is no viable solution.

Professional consultation from outside the company would be expensive, probably not worth the money. Alan would be asked to analyse his own position. The consultant might steer Alan in the right direction, but Alan would have done the real work, and taken the hard decision.

It is hardly surprising that after weighing up these alternatives, Alan chose the first option – to sort it out for himself.

He sat down one Sunday morning at home and reviewed the situation as dispassionately as he could. He was a professional manager, trained to prepare a financial audit. This process was not much different.

*T*HEORY

We all need to review our positions from time to time. We can do this by looking at our:

The key point about a SWOT analysis is that it reviews both internal factors – our personal strengths and weaknesses – and external factors – opportunities and threats.

The exercise must be approached in an honest and down-to-earth way. Alan found it a rewarding experience because he was both objective and positive in his self-appraisal. This is what he wrote:

My Strengths

1 A wealth of experience of the job.
2 Good temperament. Don't panic.
3 Considerable knowledge of the company and the computer industry in general.
4 Professional in my approach to the job and always reliable.
5 I have a sound grasp of the wider issues of management.
6 Good people-management. I am known to be sound. Someone to be relied on.

Opportunities

1 Company in a mess. They need someone with my expertise and political acumen.
2 Matthew is not as good at the job as everyone thinks he is. He hasn't got sufficient experience.
3 Stuart Blyth hasn't got a natural right-hand person yet. He's going to need one.
4 Financial control is going to be more important than ever – the banks will see to that.
5 The biggest problems in the short-term are going to be in marketing – so I have some time on my side.

My Weaknesses

1 My age.

2 Too set in my ways. Unwilling to change things.
3 I'm not assertive enough. Can't say 'No'.

4 I don't hide my feelings about the new management.

5 I talk too much about the old days and Duncan Johnson.
6 I get tired easily.

Threats

1 Matthew.

2 Vulcan could collapse and I won't get another good job now.

3 The computer world is changing all the time and it's a young person's game.
4 I have no natural ally in the company – they've all left.

5 I don't think the existing management team is good enough to save Vulcan.

The analysis revealed to Alan that the positives outweighed the negatives. He realized just how much he still had to offer the company.

He now needed to devise a marketing strategy to promote these qualities. This he boiled down to three questions:

1 ▶ Where am I now?

Alan had established this by writing his own SWOT analysis. He realized quite simply that Stuart needed help – and that he could be the man to provide it.

2 ▶ Where am I going?

This would be his new strategy. He would try to take some of the load off Stuart and effectively become his deputy. At the same time this would enable Matthew to take over some of Alan's work and save face all round.

3 ▶ How am I going to get there?

He now had to work out his tactics. He was going to prove to Stuart that he was an effective manager who still had much to offer.

He chose to play to his strengths – experience and reliability – while at the same time reducing his weaknesses. He would stop talking about the 'good old days' and he would even consider going on an assertiveness training course.

Most of all, he realized that for once in his life he would have to be devious. He had to make sure that Matthew did not succeed at his expense.

Alan believed that he now had the blueprint for success, and for the first time in years he was actually looking forward to going back to work on Monday. (Reg Owen, Matthew's number two in accounts, was going to play an essential role in Alan's plan. *See case study 3).*

*E*XERCISE

Prepare your own action plan.

1 State clearly your personal objectives: 'To...', followed by an action word. Don't be woolly. Writing it down is the only way to give your objective sufficient definition.

2 Be clear how your objective will look in action. What will you actually be doing more effectively for yourself?

3 When you want to achieve this, and how it will help you/other people/the organization in practical terms?

4 Check whether any of your objectives conflict with each other.

5 Identify any forces in your favour which will help to achieve your objective:

(a) External (the organization, other people)

(b) Internal (arising from within yourself)

6 Identify any forces against your objective.

(a) External

(b) Internal

7 How can you strengthen the forces in your favour and weaken the forces against?

8 When you have put your plan into action, reward yourself with a pleasant task, or with some time off.

DEALING WITH A DISGRUNTLED SUBORDINATE

> Oh, wad some power the giftie gie us
> to see oursels as others see us
> Robert Burns, Scottish national poet

Reg Owen was not a happy man. Vulcan's senior bookkeeper had virtually been promised the job of chief accountant last year by financial director Alan Dawson. And then came the news that an outsider, Matthew Davies, had been appointed to replace the now-retired chief accountant. Reg was forced to swallow his pride. He had a home loan to pay and jobs were not plentiful.

He found himself growing to resent Matthew. The fact that Matthew was young and had been to a top university added salt to the wounds. Reg was 45 and had no real qualifications. He felt vulnerable. Worse, he knew some of his colleagues were smirking behind his back. Matthew was completely oblivious to the problem and when it finally dawned on him how much his second in command resented him he simply did not know how to handle it.

Reg had been quick to spot Matthew's Achilles' heel. Matthew was struggling with Alan's somewhat archaic credit control system which demanded considerable knowledge of the differing arrangements Vulcan had with over 2,000 accounts. Matthew upset some important customers when he tried to improve the system and Reg simply could not resist the chance to undermine his boss at the weekly meetings which Alan chaired.

There were thinly veiled sarcastic remarks like: "I hope we aren't going to send the debt collectors around to any more of our best clients this week." Alan was rather enjoying the situation. He liked to see the young whizz kid struggling but he warned Matthew after one meeting: "You've got to stop Reg showing you up like that. He's going to undermine your position completely if you let him get away with it." Matthew decided to have a quiet face-to-face meeting with Reg to clear the air once and for all. They met one lunchtime at a local bar and Matthew said: "Look Reg, I know you're annoyed at being passed over. But it's not my fault, it was Alan who didn't keep his promise. Sulking isn't going to solve anything. Why don't you swallow your pride and try and work with me? I'm sure we can do it."

But the wound was too deep. Reg shuffled his feet, avoided Matthew's gaze and mumbled: "I don't know what you're talking about, there's no problem." Matthew realized that he had a major problem. What should he do about Reg?

Matthew was aware that he had several options open to him:

1 ▶ Ask Alan to reprimand Reg personally.

Verdict   By asking Alan to intervene, Matthew would have been made to look unfit for management. Making the problem an official disciplinary issue might well have given Reg the right to appeal to the next level up in the hierarchy; in other words, the managing director. Matthew should not risk creating such a situation. This was his first major test and he knew he had to handle it without Alan's help.

2 ▶ Give Reg a formal warning himself.

Verdict   This would be difficult as Reg felt he had a genuine grievance and had not really done anything wrong. A few snide remarks do not really warrant such action.

3 ▶ Quietly warn Reg that if he persisted with his current attitude he would be forced to downgrade him.

Verdict This might work but if Reg simply denied there was a problem, Matthew would have no fall-back position. The issue would be swept under the carpet but the resentment could well have been made 'official' and any future disagreements with Reg would be much more difficult to handle.

4 ▶ Ignore the problem in the short term but make sure he got even with Reg once he had established himself at Vulcan.

Verdict Matthew is not a skilled schemer. Also, he had the difficulty of working in a relatively small company. The political solution could well be easier in a large company where privacy is sometimes possible and where those who don't fit can be 'exiled' or moved sideways.

5 ▶ Bide his time, knowing that it wouldn't be long before he learnt the intricacies of Vulcan's credit control system and Reg would be left with no ammunition.

Verdict This is a possible solution and workable under many circumstances. If it did not work, Matthew could, after an interval, resort to 2. But in this case, Alan had brought the problem out into the open, and Matthew had to tackle it.

6 ▶ Forestall the problem entirely by putting Reg into in an area where there would be no day-to-day conflict. By being honest with Reg at the same time, but informally, he could set Reg a challenge.

Verdict

This is what Matthew did. He already knew that he and Reg could not work together as a team, and he understood that Reg felt the same way. People you dislike seldom like you and no amount of 'soft soap' does any more than lose you credibility. Matthew suggested that Reg be appointed credit control manager:

"Your local knowledge is invaluable, Reg. You've made me realize that it will take me ages to master this system. I would like you to take on the day-to-day responsibility for credit control. I'm going to put a notice up saying that this role has added responsibilities in line with its importance to Vulcan in the present economic climate. It's an area that will give you scope and will get me out of your hair. How do you feel about that?"

Reg understood and agreed and Matthew closed the interview with a hint:

"By the way, I don't think there is any need for me to appoint a new number two just yet, I'll just wait and see how the new system works out."

Matthew had moved a long way. First he had sorted out his credit control headache. Secondly, by giving Reg a specific job where he was much less likely to develop further resentment, he had not only reduced the chance of further public scenes, but also allowed Reg to develop. The closing remark that the post of a new number two was not to be filled immediately also gave Reg a target, without promising anything.

Matthew's plan worked. Reg respected his new boss. He enjoyed the chance to develop his ideas on improving the credit control system.

Alan had also been impressed. Matthew made sure that there were no serious repercussions by telling Alan what he was planning to do. "I'm thinking of shifting Reg to credit control for a while. There's no problem with that, is there?"

Alan, rather grudgingly, had to admit there was not – for the time being, at least.

THEORY

Reduce the negative factors and increase the positives.
Bad procedures need to be pruned and worthwhile activities need to be improved and more effectively rewarded. Reg as a rival had to be removed. Reg as a positive force had to be nourished and pressed into service.

Matthew had to expect:

▼ **Resistance to change.**
All forced change is resented, and the more autonomy staff can be given during the process of change, the more quickly the resentment will evaporate. Matthew found that in his first months he was avoided in the company canteen and had to eat by himself. But he persisted and gradually business conversations over coffee developed into invitations to join colleagues for lunch.

▼ **Suspicion**
New managers do have a track record of getting rid of people, cutting costs, destroying private succession plans and other personal interests. Matthew is no different.

▼ **Predecessors gaining haloes**
The manager before Matthew had grown rusty and had allowed bad practices to prosper, but he was also well liked. His children went to the same school as Reg's. In immediate retrospect Matthew's predecessor was perfect. Matthew will

know that he has finally arrived when someone admits that the past was not entirely rosy.

▼ **A redistribution of the informal command network.**

Matthew will find certain people he is better able to work with than others and this 'élite' will assume a new status in the department – good or bad. Matthew's élite will certainly be different to those favoured by his predecessor. They may be chosen on personal grounds – Matthew empathizes with the younger members. The new élite will certainly be skilled. Matthew needs numerate people who are not afraid of computers. These people will get more of his time and the 'excellent bookkeepers' correspondingly less.

Matthew has to:

Plan carefully.

Lead by example.

Use open discussion with his staff.

Negotiate clear objectives, standards and targets with all his staff on an individual basis.

▶ **He needs to Plan, Do and Review.**

CHECKLIST

When you are taking over a new department:

- What are your objectives?

- What are those of the organization?

To achieve these objectives:

- What in general should be your strategy?

What are the good points in the current way of doing things?

- How do I capitalize on these?

- How do I make them better?

What are the bad points?

- How do I prioritize what needs to change?

- How do I repair the damage already done?

COPING WITH A DISSATISFIED BOSS

> Habit is...not to be flung out of the window by any man,
> but coaxed downstairs a step at a time
>
> Mark Twain

Stuart Blyth was becoming exasperated. He had only been at Vulcan Computers as managing director for three months and already he was finding Helen impossible to work with.

"I've got enough problems without her rambling memos," he muttered to his secretary.

Stuart's predecessor, Duncan Johnson, had appreciated being kept in constant touch with developments by Helen. "I really look forward to reading your personnel memos," he used to say at their weekly meetings. "They help me keep my finger on the pulse of the company."

That was why Helen was completely mystified by Stuart's response. Hadn't he said he wanted to be kept informed about staff changes when he first joined the company? And now after three months he had finally snapped and thrown back her latest memo: "Don't keep sending me these boring reports. I just haven't got time to read this stuff."

What had Helen done wrong ?

She had simply failed to understand her new boss. She was convinced he was wrong about her reports; but he was the boss. It was up to her to put the situation right.

She considered the options open to her:

1   1 Discuss the problem with her colleagues. Perhaps some of them had also experienced the same problem and found a solution.

2   2 She could go and discuss it with Stuart and ask him which system of communication he preferred.

3   3 She could send fewer and shorter memos in future.

Any one of these three options could have worked with varying degrees of success, but Helen was a resourceful woman.

She happened to know the personnel manager at Stuart's previous company. So she rang her up and invited her for a drink.

Half way through the conversation she casually asked what sort of memo system Stuart had used in his previous company.

"He hates memos," was the reply. "Stuart was famous for throwing out the old system. He hates written communications, he much prefers oral reports. I just used to ring him up if there was a major problem. He enjoys a good joke. The only trouble is, once you get him on the phone, you can't get him to shut up."

THEORY

All bosses are different. Some like to have regular formal meetings in the office; others like to get away and talk things over informally after work. Some are avid readers of memos; others prefer two-minute conversations.

Your boss's valued skills (*case study 5*) might be completely different to yours. Some bosses are task-oriented, others are more concerned with issues of control, others with personal relationships. If you don't come to terms with the essential working style of your boss, it may not be too long before he or she takes a dislike to you.

Don't despair if your boss's style conflicts with yours. You can find other ways to express your valued skills with other colleagues and subordinates.

You have to accept the fact of office politics and you might need to become more of a political animal if you are to survive.

Information about your boss is therefore essential. You might find yourself on the receiving end of widely varying opinions about your superior, but in the end you must trust your own judgement.

There are five basic steps to take:

1 Get to understand the pressures which affect your boss. It could be that his or her boss is a tyrant; he may be involved in a vicious power struggle with one of his rivals; his marriage might be on the rocks. You need to know his standing in the company.

Once you have identified these pressures, it will make it easier for you to accept the unfair demands he makes on you from time to time.

2 ▶ Find out how often your boss needs to meet you face-to- face.

3 ▶ As a general rule, key information should be reported in as short a form as possible and on a regular basis – say, once a month. This helps to guard against poor memory being an acceptable excuse for not acting on important information.

4 ▶ Which tone of voice puts your boss at ease? Does he/she like everything to be on a first-name basis or to be addressed by a formal title? Nearly all bosses prefer respectful tones, so at first err on the side of caution.

5 ▶ Find out all the little idiosyncrasies that make your boss tick as a human being. Does she dislike people smoking in public? Is he especially intolerant of long lunches?

You may need to learn more about your own and your superior's psychological needs when it comes to social contact.

The questionnaire following, compiled from several sources, notably the psychologists Maslow and Schultz, may help. Its basis is that people satisfy their personal needs at work in two main ways – the achievement of the task itself and contact with others. The needs we satisfy from contact with others can be split down further: belonging to the group; having a role in the group; and relating to individuals.

The questions can be filled in as if you were a subordinate, or a boss.

A total of ten points must be distributed between the options in each question. Thus Question 1 might be scored: **a** *= 3,* **b** *= 0,* **c** *= 2,* **d** *= 5, to give a total of ten.*

Question *1*

When you/your boss gets into the office:

a Is it straight down to work? ☐

b Do you/they want to find out what everyone has been doing the previous day? ☐

c Do you/they check on whether instructions have been carried out? ☐

d Is it an informal conversation with a lieutenant or colleague? ☐

Question *2*

When there is an invitation to a firm's social get-together:

a Is it a chore? Are there are better and more useful things to do? ☐

b Do you/your boss look forward to it? ☐

c Is it likely that you/your boss is organizing part of it anyway? ☐

d You/your boss hope to renew some old acquaintances? ☐

Question *3*

When you/your boss starts working in a large group:

a Do you/your boss get into a corner and try to get on with the work while they argue or talk? ☐

b Do you/your boss worry until it is quite clear that you/they belong to the group? ☐

c Do you/your boss feel uncomfortable until it is clear what is required of them, or get down to restoring order from the chaos? ☐

d Do you/your boss look around for friendly faces? ☐

Question 4

When you or your boss is away from base:

a Do you/your boss hope that the clear instructions left will be adequate and followed? ☐

b Do you/your boss expect to feel a little left out of it when you return? ☐

c Do you/your boss make regular checks to see that things are on course? ☐

d Do you/they delegate to a trusted lieutenant and exchange long phone calls? ☐

Question 5

If you/they are invited to present work to a large meeting or conference:

a Do you/they concentrate on the written presentation? ☐

b Do you/they get most concerned with the oral presentation, perhaps rehearsing it in front of a group or a TV camera? ☐

c Do you/they get involved with the organization? ☐

d Do you/your boss look forward to the informal discussion after work? ☐

The total should add up to 50.

	Your total	Your boss's total
a		
b		
c		
d		

The **a** total is about *task*. Helen had an a total of 25 and her boss, in her opinion, only had 14. This does not mean that her boss, Stuart, was not concerned with the task, but that he had other needs.

The **b** total is about *wanting to identify with a group*. Both Helen and Stuart were low in this, scoring five and six respectively.

The **c** total is about *needing a role* and about *a need for clarity*. Both Helen and Stuart had a middle score of 12. Stuart needed clarity from Helen and Helen required clarity to work effectively. There were no problems there.

The **d** total is about *the need to recognize and be recognized as an individual*. Here lay Helen's problem. Stuart had a score of 18 and Helen eight. Where Stuart wanted to see/talk directly with Helen so that he could feel how things were going, Helen had been presenting him with 'cold' memos.

ADAPTING THE JOB
TO YOUR SKILLS

I have room in my army for hard working intelligent officers. And I have
room in my army for lazy intelligent officers – in fact they often make
the best. I even have room in my army for lazy unintelligent officers.
But I have no room in my army for hard working unintelligent officers.

Napoleon Bonaparte

Betty Jones thrived on a crisis. She admitted that she found it boring when everything was running smoothly, and nobody could ever accuse her marketing department of lacking excitement.

Betty had a habit of leaving things to the last minute, or even worse. Two years ago she had changed the layout of Vulcan's stand on the eve of a trade fair. The effect had, at best, been described as 'dramatic'.

Betty was a constant thorn in the side of production director Campbell Ritchie, who had challenged her at a board meeting.

"These special offers you decide to push... you never warn me to increase our production runs." He added: "You just don't consider how much extra work it puts on my staff."

Betty's reply was predictable: "Selling is the lifeblood of this company. If we can't sell the computers there's no point in making them."

Sometimes Betty had disasters, but her successes far outweighed her failures. One of her most notable triumphs was a large export order to Italy, when Betty had delivered the order herself.

The whole Italian order had been on a tight but realistic schedule – the computers had to be delivered within four weeks – and the consignment reached the transporters on time thanks to the energetic efforts of Campbell and his production staff.

Things had gone wrong after factory despatch and Betty was the first to hear. She had been woken at home on Sunday morning and told that the truck driver had been taken ill in northern France and the co-driver had abandoned the cargo. Betty promptly found another driver, and together they flew immediately to Paris. They drove the consignment to Turin overnight and beat the deadline. The story made the national press.

Betty considered this to be a high point in her career, and was not shy of saying so.

Do you agree?

*T*HEORY

Betty did what most managers try to do – she moulded her daily work so that she could use those skills which she personally valued.

She enjoyed the unexpected, and derived immediate satisfaction from the way in which she was able to organize and motivate people to do unusual things. She was good at co-ordinated planning under pressure.

Betty could also perform routine tasks when the need arose. But she did not enjoy working that way; she found it boring. Unfortunately, she viewed people who were methodical in their work as being boring, too.

She despised Campbell's orderly routine world and could not resist any opportunity to ruffle him. She saw Campbell as a dull manager who needed shaking up. Campbell considered her 'erratic'.

Imagine if Betty and Campbell swapped jobs. Their different styles would be completely inappropriate both for themselves and for Vulcan. Betty would get bored and engineer a crisis, whereas Campbell would hope that certain problems would go away and not interfere with the smooth running of his department.

Think back over your working life and try to identify the stages on the next page. Almost everyone goes through each of them.

Stage 1

▼

You choose a job which best fits your needs and expectations at a particular time.

Stage 2

▼

You start work and adapt your behaviour to the job.

Stage 3

▼

You start to modify the job so that you can use the skills which you value most.

Stage 4

▼

You reach a balance between your valued skills and the demands of the job.

Stage 5

▼

You, or others, decide whether the balance is valid; re-adjustments occur.

*E*XERCISE

Think of two incidents when you acted as a manager and which you recall with pride.

Don't limit your choice to formal management situations. For instance, it could include working with a youth group or even helping at the scene of an accident.

You ought to be able to look back on the incidents with pleasure and say to yourself: 'I derived real satisfaction from using my skills.'

Decide which skills you used and why they gave you satisfaction.

Now look at your present job. Divide your work into areas of responsibility, listing the different skills required for each area. Give a simple rating for the importance of that skill – either high, medium or low.

Look at the list from two different points of view – first, as though you were an independent assessor; secondly, to discover how you personally value your skills.

If there is a large discrepancy between the two, you probably need to adjust. For instance, an independent assessor might rate initiative as low, whereas you might rate it as high. If this is the case, you may have to curb your natural instinct to do things on your own.

At the other extreme, you may rate teamwork as high, but the assessor might rate it as low. In which case you probably ought to try being more of a self-starter.

If you cannot bridge the gap between the two views, you should take a long hard look at your career plans.

AVOIDING CONFRONTATION

Delay is preferable to error
Thomas Jefferson, third President of the U.S.A.

Alan Dawson had been expecting a confrontation, either with Matthew Davies or with Stuart Blyth, Matthew's champion. Alan knew it would not be long before Matthew tried to flex his muscles by insisting to Stuart that Alan give him greater authority.

Alan was known as Vulcan's Mr Nice Guy and always had great difficulty in saying 'No' to his colleagues. This time, however, he was determined to resist any attempts at undermining his authority at Vulcan.

But he had not anticipated that the crunch would come so quickly. One morning, he was called in to Stuart's office:

"Alan, you know that Reg Owen has taken some of the workload off Matthew in credit control – well, I think it's time we gave Matthew a chance to prepare the monthly financial reports. I know that you have done a good job on these in the past, but I think we need some fresh ideas. That's why I want Matthew to start work on this project straight away."

Alan saw it as the beginning of the end: Matthew taking over his job.

What would you do if you were Alan?

1 Flatly refuse to hand over a key area currently under your control? After all, you are the financial director and Matthew is only the company's chief accountant.

Verdict Quite right – but for how long could you survive on this basis? There is no use in antagonising Stuart. You might win this particular battle, but maybe you would not win the war.

2 Give in.

Verdict You might as well throw away this book. Good managers don't give in so easily.

3 Try to seek a compromise.

Verdict Yes – but how? Alan has been taken by surprise. Stuart wants to push his plan through, regardless of Alan's protests.

Alan's first priority must be to keep cool and give himself time in which to think.

The difficulty was Stuart's persistence:

"I want this to happen, Alan. I've got faith in Matthew and I think you could do with his help. He's prepared a report making various recommendations to improve our existing financial reporting system and I've been very impressed."

Alan knew that the only answer was for him to buy time. He couldn't think clearly in Stuart's office. He was upset, there was no denying that, but he couldn't allow that to colour his judgement.

He replied as calmly and as slowly as he could.

"I'm glad that Matthew has some good ideas. What I would like to do now is read his report."

"Look, I don't think you heard me, I want Matthew to start on this right away."

"I would like a few minutes to read the report and then I can get back to you."

"Look, Alan, the report isn't the real issue."

"I would still like to read the report."

"We haven't got much time."

"I still need a few minutes to read the report."

Alan was resisting pressure and buying time through the use of a technique known as **broken record**. It means:

- Deciding on a position.

- Using a level voice.

- Not being afraid to say the same thing, over and over again.

- Not being drawn and not answering questions.

"Alan, this is important, I need to know if you are going to co-operate with Matthew on this project – I need an immediate response now."

"I realize you would like an immediate response, but I still need time to understand what has to be done."

Alan is still not moving from his prepared position. He is now using another technique – **fielding** – for taking the sting out of pressure.

It involves:

> ● Listening to what the other person says.
>
> ● Acknowledging what you have heard, using some of the same words.
>
> ● Accepting that others have a right to their opinion.
>
> ● Accepting the truth, however small, in what they say.
>
> ● And once again maintaining your position by means of broken record.

You do not have to defend, blame or justify. Just stay with the technique and keep your cool.

Stuart did not enjoy bashing his head against a brick wall and he began to suspect that he had under-estimated Alan.

Alan continued: "I realize you would like an immediate response but I still need some time to understand what has to be done. Why don't you let me read Matthew's report in my office? We can discuss it over lunch."

"You realize the importance – OK, lunchtime. But we won't go into the cafeteria. How about the local Chinese restaurant?"

Alan and Stuart were on their way to reaching a **workable compromise**. Stuart was not an unreasonable boss and he admired the way Alan handled what was obviously a stressful situation. Over lunch, Alan had the time to tell Stuart that he believed staff down the line can have good new ideas and improved ways of analysing and presenting information; but that artful

management means bringing out their ideas –
without allowing the senior manager's position to
be undermined in the process.

"Give Matthew total control of the monthly
reports, and you give him a slice of my job," said
Alan. "Let me judge his proposals objectively,
and take aboard the best of them; then I'll be
giving proper value for my salary."

Stuart could not disagree. It turned out that the
three of them agreed to implement some, but
not all, of Matthew's proposals. Matthew would
help Alan prepare the monthly reports while still
leaving Alan in overall charge. In the meantime
Matthew would start monitoring special projects
which were not included in the monthly reports.

Workable compromises are not always
possible, but this one was possible because:

> ● Alan successfully resisted the initial
> pressure.
>
> ● He searched for, and found, concessions
> that Matthew (and Alan) could live with, which
> did not undermine his position.
>
> ● Alan got his timing right; he acted as the
> problem arose.

*T*HEORY

The simple techniques of broken record, fielding
and workable compromise are quite easy to
remember and to put into effect. They can be
used at work or at home, helping you to act
appropriately when under pressure.

Broken record and fielding are, of course,
ploys for buying time: time in which to think in
a clear-headed way, avoiding knee-jerk reactions
which one so often regrets afterwards. It is
frustrating, in situations such as Alan's, to have
to deny oneself the release of righteous anger. But
in the workplace, success depends more on
action than emotion. The best approach is not to
get mad, but to get even.

In any case, you are never at your most
effective when feeling churned up by insult or
injustice.

*E*XERCISE

Think back on stressful situations which you
have had to deal with.

How much better would you have done if
you had used the techniques described in this
case study?

Now think ahead to the next time you will
find yourself under stress; rehearse your
application of the techniques.

SELF-MARKETING STRATEGY

A man is known by the company he organizes
Ambrose Bierce

Stuart stayed at a local hotel for his first three weeks at Vulcan while he and his wife Monica looked for a new house. Vulcan did not have an account at the motel, and so none of the staff knew who Stuart was. He soon discovered that the place was a useful source of local commercial gossip. One evening he overheard this conversation between two customers.

"Apparently the new boss at Vulcan is a miserable type. Always moaning about how tough it's going to be. The attitude rubs off on to everyone else and they're all getting depressed."

"It's mushroom management – they keep the staff in the dark and throw bullshit all over them," was the rejoinder.

"So that's it," mused Stuart. Clearly, he had failed to market himself and his new ideas for Vulcan properly. He was constantly 'selling' himself to the external customers – the banks, suppliers, distributors and retailers, but he had virtually ignored his internal customers. He had given a pep talk to the whole workforce on arrival and he did make a point of seeing his managers as often as he could. Evidently, this had not been enough.

Stuart needed his own self-marketing plan, and he set about preparing it, none the less worried that he had missed the best time to implement it – the honeymoon period following his arrival in the new job.

*T*HEORY

There is one rule for self-marketing: ignore the motto 'Begin as you mean to go on.' You must be flexible in your approach. As with most other managerial activities, there are three stages:

- Plan
- Do
- Review

The planning stage means analysing your objectives. What do you think Stuart's objectives should be? Write down a list of ten. How do they compare with the list below?

1 Gain acceptance from the staff.

2 Win their respect.

3 Build and maintain an effective team.

4 Help to develop the individuals within that team.

5 Build on existing strengths.

6 Get rid of the dead wood in other areas and start again with fresh people.

7 Improve his own career path.

8 Get an interesting new project off the ground.

Breaking down priorities into a list may seem pedantic, but it is the only way to ensure that your analysis of objectives is specific, rather than woolly. Having defined your goals as clearly as this, it is then equally important to sum them up in an overview.

Stuart's overview was simple. To get Vulcan back on its feet, he had to improve the management team dramatically. If this could be done, the team would motivate the workforce below them to perform better.

Selling this goal to the existing management and employees was, he realized, easier said than done. There was no disguising the fact that to 'improve' meant not only to strengthen his existing staff, but to cut away dead wood. Stuart faced the perennial top manager's dilemma: he wanted to be popular, but he had to do some unpopular things. He wanted to sell himself as a boss committed to preserving people in their jobs; but was bound to invite the charge of insincerity because everyone knew that sooner or later he would wield the axe.

If Stuart began communicating his plans for Vulcan to his managers on an individual basis, he had therefore to expect suspicion and apprehension; perhaps also resentment and resistance to change. If a manager felt threatened, he or she might well defend his or her position by trying to look into Stuart's own track record for evidence that he had been ruthless with people's jobs, yet failed to produce results. This would seriously undermine his position – were it true.

Faced with this situation, the chief executive needs to know how each manager is likely to react as she sells them her plans for the future. This can take some of the anxiety and uncertainty out of the situation. In the case of Vulcan's

existing management team, Stuart predicted that
by no means all of them would react badly. Alan
might be suspicious; Betty, by contrast, disliked
the previous M.D. and would see Stuart as an
opportunity. Thinking about each individual's
likely reactions made him realize that he could
broach difficult topics without uniting the team
against him in suspicion and fear.

But how exactly to go about it?

Implementing a self-marketing plan

Impromptu pep talks are not recommended.
Inherited groups of managers know each other,
and have informal means of communication. The
new chief executive must control the way plans
are divulged; managers must not learn about
them in advance: they must be presented in their
best light, and the chief executive has this as his
or her responsibility.

Stuart Blyth's method was to summon each of
the managers individually, in rapid succession, for
an initial, relaxed interview in which he outlined
his plans for the business.

In these discussions, he was able to sense the
commitment of each manager and begin the
process of establishing trust, essential to any
management team. At the start of each interview
he said that he was telling the manager his plans
because he needed to know what he or she felt;
at the end he asked them to go away and reflect
on what they had heard, requesting a date when
they could come back for a second meeting to tell
him their views. He also emphasized that at the
end of the day the final decision would be his.

As a result, the management team could not
complain that they were being ignored; and most
of them avoided comparing notes after the first
interview because they wanted credit for their
own ideas when they went back for the second.

By implying that he did not necessarily need their approval for his plans, Stuart made it clear that he did not intend to abdicate authority; that he would accept even unpopularity if push came to shove.

At the same time, he was making it clear, by sharing the information and inviting their views, that he wanted commitment, and would not lightly risk unpopularity.

This balance is an essential rule of management, and if it can be achieved the benefits will quite quickly percolate down through the organization grapevine, improving morale.

*E*XERCISE

Imagine that you are taking over a new group.

● Analyse your objectives.

● Analyse the reactions from individuals.

● Rehearse the introduction to your strategy for the first and second meetings.

GOOD DAYS, BAD DAYS

> My wife was immature.
> When I was in the bath, she'd come and sink my boats
> Woody Allen

Campbell Ritchie, Vulcan's production director, saw himself, on what his wife called his good days, as a hard but fair manager with a sound grasp of what his job was about: carrying out board policy. He was good at taking instructions and issuing firm directives to his juniors. He accepted that part of his job was understanding, and being genuinely concerned about, his staff. He could dispense justice with mercy. He also saw himself as essentially reasonable, capable of justifying and explaining any of his actions.

He was less good at company politics, and at manipulating people, preferring straightforward roles, clear objectives, defined responsibilities and people who were ready and able to get on with the job.

When under stress, Campbell changed from the tough-but-fair manager into a recluse. He was unaware that colleagues had noticed this trait until he overheard a conversation in the works cafeteria between two of his supervisors. The previous day had been a difficult one for Campbell, and in the late afternoon he had decided that he needed to stop and think things out. He had thought, quite reasonably in his view, that it would be best for him to lose his bleeper for about half an hour and sit in his car. His supervisors had a different view.

"The man is never there when you need him," said Jim Smith.

"The usual?" asked George Baker.

"The usual. The whole of Process Room Number Two was down because of the quality scare. What was I supposed to do with the operators? Send them home? I needed Campbell to tell me how soon it could be fixed. Where was he? He was in his car listening to his blessed CD player. Bleeper off, of course."

"Did you try to get him out?"

"No way. You can't disturb him when he's buried in his Mozart. He's fine when things are right, but when things go wrong..."

Campbell had to admit to himself, with some discomfort, that they were right. Looking back on the day, he realized that although the solutions he developed in his half hour of battery recharging had been excellent, he had, during that period, forgotten his prime job: being a manager. Anything could have happened while he was out of touch.

Can you think of ways in which Campbell could get over his problem in the future?

Option One

Campbell might, with considerable strain on his nervous system, resist the temptation to hide, keep his bleeper on and wade in to solve the problem.

Verdict

A robot cannot solve a problem for which it is not programmed; nor can Campbell. Campbell cannot handle situations which will not yield to his natural management style, which is strong on direction, caring and logic, but weak on manipulation.

On a bad day, Campbell finds that even this natural balance breaks down, and he loses his ability to direct and to care; virtually all his energy goes into logic: he finds he needs to 'think things out'. His staff want direction and care all the time; Campbell cannot give these when he is stressed. This is a real problem, intrinsic to Campbell's make-up, and it cannot just be 'overcome'.

Option Two

> Campbell could explain to his supervisors that, when he is under stress, he needs time to think things out. Then at least they could have some warning.

Verdict

Bad for Campbell, and bad for his supervisors. The 'warning' would be seen as a public admission of inadequacy; and Campbells's staff would still be landed with a crisis difficult to solve without direction. Something better is needed.

Option Three

> Go some way towards solving the problem – as far as Campbell can manage, at any rate – as soon as he gets the early warning signs of stress. These, in Campbell's (and in most people's) experience are easy to recognize – Campbell's symptom was a glowing feeling in the arms and legs.
>
> When early warnings appeared, he could find himself a quiet place to talk to a trusted subordinate and review immediate action to stop the situation getting out of hand; but not attempt, at this stage, to solve the problem.

Verdict

This is not a perfect solution; but none of us are perfect people. At least it accomodates Campbell's need for time to think with his staff's need to know what they should do next.

*T*HEORY

Everyone has 'sides' to their personalities. In management, behaviour is determined by how we balance four key sides of the personality:

● **Controlling,** and its opposite, **being controlled.**

● **Caring** for others or the opposite, **being dependent on others.**

● **Working through problems** by logic or the opposite, by **intuition.**

● Being **'political'** or manipulative or the opposite, being **naive.**

Campbell's psychological balance can be shown in a diagram representing these poles of behaviour.

	GOOD DAY	BAD DAY
CONTROLLING	✓	
BEING CONTROLLED		✓
CARING FOR OTHERS	✓	
BEING DEPENDENT ON OTHERS		✓

Campbell is quite high on control on a good day, but less so on a bad one. The pattern is similar on the 'caring for others/being dependent on others' axis.

	GOOD DAY	BAD DAY
WORKING ON LOGIC		✓
RELYING ON INTUITION	✓	

The big switch comes on this axis. On a good day he does things intuitively; on a bad day he becomes extremely logical. (This is a characteristic of many engineers – they like to go back to the drawing board.)

	GOOD DAY	BAD DAY
BEING POLITICAL	✓	
BEING NAIVE		✓

Campbell is not normally a political animal; and on a bad day he forgets to 'look after his back' completely.

*E*XERCISE

Draw a diagram of your own behaviour and consider the problems that behavioural changes can cause. Even quite minor changes can be unnerving for colleagues, especially those who have recently come into your orbit.

One form of personality change is particularly common: caring under normal circumstances, the manager under stress often becomes cold and unsympathetic. Juniors can find this completely disorienting, and it may make them wary of the manager for ever after.

Or perhaps you recognize, having analysed the pattern in cold blood, that you lose your political antennae when under stress. Remember that this is when astute competitors will pounce.

You cannot change your personality overnight, but a cold stare at your switching tendencies will probably limit the damage.

COMMUNICATING
WELL

EFFECTIVE COMMUNICATION

> I apologise for the length of this letter,
> but I didn't have time to write a short one
> Winston Churchill

Stuart realized, soon after his arrival, that the lines of communication at Vulcan were inadequate. The five senior managers he had inherited were not on his wavelength. Worse still, they did not seem capable of communicating with each other. He made a mental note to himself of each individual's faults:

ALAN (finance)	Tends to waffle. He is trying too hard to please me and he just rambles on, never getting to the point.
BETTY (marketing)	Is far too hasty. She won a major contract while last month's financial report was being written by Alan and Matthew. She just forgot to tell them about it. She needs to give herself, and everyone else around her, more breathing space.
HELEN (personnel)	Makes everything sound complicated. She is trying to improve her department but gets bogged down in theory. There are far too many terms, such as 'psychometric profiles', which the others don't understand.
CAMPBELL (production)	Writes reports that are bound to be technical, but nevertheless are still far too long-winded and detailed. I dread having to read them.
MATTHEW (new boy finance)	Uses a shotgun approach. He peppers every concept with random facts. Some hit the target, most of them miss. He seems to think that just because he finds a certain topic interesting, everyone else will share his enthusiasm.

Stuart knew that his options were limited. He could not hold a board meeting and itemise each manager's failings in front of the others. Obviously, he needed to have a quiet word with each of them to point out individual problems.

Can you think of a tactful, and simple, point you could put to each of these managers that would make them aware of their deficiencies and help them to be better communicators in future?

THEORY

There are five basic rules of effective communication.

1 ▶ Know what you want to say before saying it. If this means re-thinking basic objectives, so much the better. Alan's objective was to win Stuart's confidence, but he never reminded himself of this before speaking. Nor did he rehearse what he had to say.

> *Stuart told Alan:* "Please be more specific from now on. I appreciate what you have to say, but we can both give more time to the important issues if you refine everything down to the key points."

2 ▶ Allow a margin of time in which to communicate: Betty seemed incapable of working to a deadline and she did not appreciate that she had a responsibility to inform others of her activities.

> *Stuart told Betty:* "Slow down, allow some breathing space in your day so that you can get colleagues up to date with your actions."

3 ▶ Keep it simple: Helen was becoming increasingly effective as a manager, but she was in danger of spoiling it all by over-elaboration.

> *Stuart told Helen:* "Get back to basics. You are spoiling your message by using complex terms when simple ones will do."

5 ▶ Keep it short: Campbell had verbal diarrhoea. His reports would be far more effective if they were cut by at least half.

> *Stuart told Campbell:* "Your reports should start with a summary which tells me the essentials without my reading the whole report. This summary should be almost as much trouble to write as the rest of the report."

4 ▶ Aim at your audience: Matthew was writing reports without asking himself what the readers needed to know. He needed to differentiate between what was relevant to the bank and what was relevant to the other managers.

> *Stuart told Matthew:* "Make sure that the person receiving your report actually needs that information."

Most of us find it relatively easy to adhere to the first four basic rules of effective communication, but knowing your audience is harder. The exercise that follows is designed to help you to be more sensitive to others' reactions to simple messages. If you can achieve the necessary level of sensitivity, you can also target your audience with improved accuracy.

EXERCISE

How will a subordinate react if you say:

Your work is	*a*	not adequate
	b	not good enough
	c	not as agreed
	d	giving me problems

or if you say:

Your work is	*a*	reasonable
	b	improving
	c	well above average
	d	excellent

How do you want them to react? Reflect on the differences between the two sets of approaches.

Helen was impressed by Betty's success in clinching the Thompson deal. She knew George Thompson was a tough negotiator and hadn't expected Vulcan to win the contract at the asking price.

"How did you do it, Betty?" she asked.

"George drives a hard bargain," replied Betty. "But his body language gave him away. I could tell that he had to buy from Vulcan at our price even though he kept saying he wouldn't. He kept sitting on the edge of his seat, so I knew he was prepared to settle. If he had been sitting back, I'd have been worried."

"Do you always rely on body language during difficult negotiations?"

"You know what they say: If all else fails you can always use words," laughed Betty. "Even with a canny operator like Stuart, there are give-away visual clues. He always avoids eye contact when he's under pressure.

"Alan's body language is actually more subtle. It can be hard to detect. But have you noticed how often he crosses his arms in front of his chest? It's a defensive posture and he does it when he anticipates attack. He also crosses his legs when he disagrees with you.

"Then there's Matthew. I think he fancies me. I've given him the cold shoulder, and whenever I'm about he scuffles along the corridor with his hands deep in his pockets, head down and shoulders hunched."

Body language involves interpretation of many kinds of gestures. Isolated gestures are like words in a sentence: you must read the word in its context to find the true meaning. Body language also changes in different parts of the world. The examples given here relate to Europe, North America, and the 'White British Commonwealth'.

Openness

It is obvious when people take their coats off, unbutton their collars, or extend their arms towards you, that they are generally beginning to feel comfortable in your presence. Less obvious gestures include open hands, moving closer towards you, leaning slightly forward in the chair and uncrossed arms and legs. These also may suggest sincerity.

Beware, however, if someone puts a leg over the arm of a chair. It might seem that he or she is relaxed and open, but in reality that person may well be inclined to drop out of the conversation. Straddling a chair might also look informal and open, but it is a latently aggressive pose, adopted by those contemplating confrontation. The back of the chair is their defensive screen, to be used when the time comes.

Defensiveness

A 'tight' posture suggests defensiveness. Everything about this person is compacted. The body is rigid, the arms and legs tightly crossed. There is minimal eye contact, lips are pursed, fists clenched and the head is downcast.

Suspicion

Sideways glances with head poised slightly downwards, minimal or no eye contact; shifting the body away from the speaker and touching or rubbing the nose. A sideways glance can register suspicion and doubt – hence the term 'cold shoulder'.

Readiness	Hands on hips reveal that someone wants to get things done and expects others to follow. Athletes preparing for a sporting event will often adopt this pose.
Reassurance	People try to reassure themselves by pinching the fleshy part of the hand, picking at fingernails, rubbing or caressing some personal object such as a pencil, pen or paper clip.
Frustration	Common gestures are tightly clenched hands; rubbing the nape of the neck, wringing the hands and running hands through hair.
Confidence	Relaxed and expansive gestures, steepling the hands; leaning back with fingers laced behind the head; hands held together behind the back, chin thrust upward.
Nervousness	Clearing the throat; covering the mouth while talking; twitching lips or face; fidgeting; shifting weight from one foot to another; tapping fingers; pacing up and down.
Self control	Tightly locking the ankles and gripping the wrists behind the back usually indicates that something is being held back.

Boredom or impatience	Drumming fingers; cupping the head in the palm of the hand; foot swinging; doodling; pointing the body towards an exit; looking at one's watch or the exit.
Enthusiasm	Eyes wide and alert; erect body; hands open and arms extended; lively, bouncy walk with a lively, well-modulated voice.
Thoughtful	Tilted head, hand to cheek, leaning forward and stroking the chin do indeed convey someone deep in thought, or someone considering what is being said in a friendly, positive manner.
	Someone who is listening critically would have their hands to their face, but the chin is in the palm of the hand with one finger going up on the cheek and the others positioned below the mouth. The body is drawn back.
	Someone who pinches the bridge of the nose, closes their eyes and slumps their head down-wards may well be inwardly locked in debate.
Positioning	Sitting behind a desk implies authority; sitting alongside someone implies the will to work with them. It is easier to argue with someone facing you than someone alongside you.

COUNSELLING –
A GENERAL STRATEGY

Look for the simple explanations first and
only if they do not work, seek to find complications.
When you have eliminated the possible, the
improbable, however impossible, is the explanation

Occam's Razor

Anne Dudley had been personal assistant to Duncan Johnson, founder and former boss of Vulcan. When Stuart agreed that she should replace Campbell's secretary, Campbell was delighted.

"She is a very neat and precise lady; and she's bound to improve the organization of the office," said Campbell. Anne began well enough, making improvements to the office lay-out and changes in stationery suppliers, but her paperwork was surprisingly sloppy and she would not accept criticism.

"I don't know why he complains so much about my typing," said Anne. "He's far too fussy. Duncan thought my letters were excellent. If they were good enough for him, I'm sure they're good enough for Campbell."

But gradually her confidence began to drain away and Campbell was forced to delegate some of her work to the other secretaries. This caused disquiet because Anne was the senior secretary, on the highest grade.

It was an awkward problem for Campbell. Anne had a sound track record within the company and he had a nagging doubt at the back of his mind that somehow he might be at fault. What should he do?

He had heard of counselling but he frankly admitted that he did not know anything about it. He discussed the matter with Helen. She told him that he had made a fundamental error in communicating with Anne:

1 ►He had failed to find out systematically what the problem might be. He had taken a few educated guesses, but he was still not sure.

2 ►He had failed to explain to Anne why she needed to change. Campbell needed a structured approach to counselling Anne. Helen advised him to adopt a four-stage strategy:

First stage: **why is there a problem and who has the problem, anyway?**
Campbell gently made Anne aware that her deteriorating work was causing problems for her boss and subordinates alike. Her boss was having a problem which very soon would become her problem – she could lose her job.

Second stage: **what is the problem?**
Could there be more than one problem? Did Anne miss working for Duncan? Did she dislike her new colleagues? Was she having difficulty with the new word processor? Was the situation being complicated by domestic difficulties?

> **The first interview**
> Campbell and Helen decided that he could only tackle one problem at a time. He and Anne would first of all focus on the least emotional issue – the word processor. Anne admitted that she preferred her old electric typewriter and was having difficulty adapting to the new equipment. Having openly identified this problem, it was simple for them to consider calmly the solutions open to them.

Third stage: **how to select a solution?**
Revert to her old typewriter? A word-processor training course? A change of job? Early retirement? Naturally, they decided that Anne needed help on the word processor.

Fourth stage: **a detailed solution.**

It was agreed that Anne should be sent on a two-week release course at a nearby training centre. When she returned they would review the position. Despite this methodical approach, Campbell was still not satisfied that they had found the real problem. Anne was a resourceful person who would not just disintegrate because she was having trouble with a new system. He knew that in due course he would have to discuss with Anne other problems which might be at the root of the trouble.

The second interview

This took place a few days after Anne's return from the course. Anne's work still had not significantly improved. Campbell did not comment on this directly, having patiently listened to what Anne thought of the course. Then he said: "Are there any other problems which you think I should know about?" There followed an uncomfortable silence (which Campbell made no attempt to fill). Then Anne revealed that she had been having trouble with her eyesight but had been too scared to go to the doctors.

Campbell quickly convinced her that she must see her doctor immediately. When she did see her doctor he told her she had a cataract on her left eye which would require an operation within three months.

Anne now found it easy to admit that poor eyesight had affected her typing and that worry about her failing vision had also reduced her general effectiveness. After the operation she quickly achieved her former high standard of work.

THEORY

Managers must expect staff to bring them personal or work problems, and to act, in response, as counsellor.

Managers generally respond in three different ways and by answering the questionnaire on the next page you will be able to identify which of these three styles you usually adopt:

● As the expert: as a MOUTH, telling the subordinate what to do.
● As a co-worker: as a PAIR OF HANDS, working with the subordinate to solve the problem.
● As a counsellor: as a PAIR OF EARS – bouncing back ideas and asking questions, but making the subordinate find out the root problem for him- or herself with a minimum of direction and guidance.

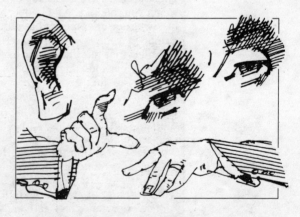

All three styles – MOUTH, HANDS and EARS – have their use in particular situations and at particular stages of the counselling process.

*E*XERCISE

Imagine that you are counselling someone with a problem. The only ways you may respond are those listed above – MOUTH, HANDS or EARS.

A total of ten points must be distributed between the options in each question. For example, your natural response in Situation one might be three for a, seven for b and zero for c.

THERE ARE NO RIGHT OR WRONG ANSWERS.

(E) stands for EARS, (H) for HANDS, and (M) for MOUTH.

Situation one
When I take on a new member of staff I tell them that:

a I like to encourage initiative. (E) ... ☐

b We are a team and everyone is expected to come up with ideas, including me. (H) ... ☐

c At the end of the day the final decision is mine. (M) ... ☐

Situation two
When my staff are facing a crisis at work I tell them that:

a I encourage a common approach to the problem within the department. (H) ... ☐

b It is my responsibility to sort things out. (M) ... ☐

c   We agree a joint strategy which
    the staff must implement. (E)   ...☐

Situation three:
When my staff are faced with personal
problems at home I tell them that:

a   Not to bring their problems
      to work. (M)   ...☐

b   To come into my office any time
      to discuss their problem. (H)   ...☐

c   I will always listen to them, but
      at the end of the day I cannot
      interfere in their private lives. (E)   ...☐

Situation four
When I give my staff some career guidance
I tell them that:

a   I am not really qualified to help.
      Their future is very much
      in their own hands. (E)   ...☐

b   I can give them some very clear
      advice. (M)   ...☐

c   Together we can analyse their
      performance and look to ways
      in which they can make
      improvements. (H)   ...☐

Situation five
When I am giving feedback to staff
I tell them that:

a   I need to know the answers
to certain key areas of
concern. (M)   ... ☐

b   Staff should ask questions
and obtain feedback. (E)   ... ☐

c   We will both take the initiative
in the matter. (H)   ... ☐

Situation six
When we are implementing a new strategy
I tell my staff that:

a   The timing of the
various stages is their
responsibility. (E)   ... ☐

b   I am here to help them
implement the strategy. (H)   ... ☐

c   I set out the timetable, as
agreed with the individual. (M) ... ☐

Transfer your scores from the check list to the scoring columns below. Add up the totals for each column. The three totals in each should add up to 60. If they do not, your balance is wrong, and it can only improve your management style to go back and try again.

	Statement (*Mouth*)	Expert (*Ears*)	Consultant Co-Worker (*Hands*)
1			
2			
3			
4			
5			
6			
TOTALS			

The effective manager acts appropriately in a whole range of situations, sometimes as the expert, sometimes as the co-worker sharing responsibility and sometimes as the consultant, leaving others to solve problems in their own way with a minimum of guidance.

THE DISCIPLINARY INTERVIEW

> Plans are nothing, planning is everything
> Dwight D Eisenhower

The sounds coming from the stock room were unmistakable. Helen's sex life was not particularly active, but she had no trouble in recognizing those noises. The door was unlocked and Helen could see the writhing, half-naked bodies of Joyce Barber and Jim Bett.

Helen felt numb. There was not much she could do about Jim Bett, who was an outside contractor, but Joyce was on her staff and had to be disciplined. She had known about this relationship for some time. Her staff had complained about it, pointing out that Bett was making far too many unnecessary visits and disrupting the smooth running of the office.

Helen told Joyce Barber to see her in her office in a quarter of an hour; then asked Jim Bett to leave the premises, adding "I'll have to consider your position later."

As the blushing couple untangled themselves, it was left to Helen to do the heavy breathing. How should she play it? When Joyce finally entered her office, it seemed as if the roles had somehow been reversed: Helen felt under pressure; Joyce seemed calm.

"You and Mr Bett were having sex on the premises."

"No we weren't, we were just fooling about, that's all."

For the second time that day Helen was taken short. She had not expected Joyce to be cheeky, or defiant. She felt like giving Joyce a formal warning, but suddenly she felt uncertain.

So she said: "I am not satisfied with your answer or your attitude. I am bringing this interview to a close. Please see me again first thing tomorrow morning."

What should Helen have done?

● Should she have simply locked the door on the couple and gone to get a witness?

● Should she have called in the police?

● Should she have called Jim Bett's boss as well?

● Should she have stayed in the store room and made them admit their guilt when they were still vulnerable?

● Should she have closed the door quietly and tiptoed away, turning a blind eye to the whole episode?

Many managers would have chosen the last option, and with some reason. But this particular relationship was common knowledge in Helen's department. In some organizations, the misconduct could have invited summary dismissal. At Vulcan it required, at the very least, a disciplinary interview.

But how to prepare for it?

*T*HEORY

In planning for a difficult meeting, you must differentiate between:

● what you must achieve, and

● what you would like to achieve.

Helen was able to distinguish between these two aims. She knew she had to discipline Joyce for disruptive behaviour. She had to prevent the relationship causing further friction and animosity in the department. *Helen knew that she MUST achieve that much.*

She also knew that she would be much happier if Joyce could admit that she and Jim Betts were using the office premises for a sexual relationship. She would like to be in a position to say that what they did in private was their affair; but that Vulcan's premises were a public place where different rules had to apply. *This was what Helen knew she would like to achieve.*

If Helen could not reach her second objective, it would be a disappointment, but not a major blow. If she did not reach her first objective, the interview would be a failure.

There were three additional points Helen needed to consider:

1 | **Practical preparation.**

Get out Joyce's personnel record file. Check up on union rules or company guidelines for such an incident. In some countries, no more than 'reasonable belief' that such an incident took place is needed to uphold dismissal. Had Helen

been ready to quote this when Joyce feigned
innocence, she might have carried the interview
through to her satisfaction.

2 │ What should she expect from Joyce?

Evasion? Defiance? Claims that the sexual
advances were unwelcome and unavoidable?

3 │ What to do afterwards?

Record the event on file. Contact Mr Bett's
company.

**How should Helen behave in the
disciplinary interview?**

In a professional manner at all times, of course.
Discipline must be fair, prompt, dispassionate
and consistent.

Fairly: The penalty must be carefully
considered according to accepted guidelines.

Promptly: Discipline must be immediate.
Delayed-action discipline sends the message,
rightly or wrongly, that management does not
take the lapse particularly seriously, or is
divided over the response.

Dispassionately: Use logical, unemotional
language. Talk as if acting against the deed,
not the doer.

EXERCISE

Imagine that you have to conduct a disciplinary interview.

1 Write down the background in simple terms: the facts as you know them; what you hear, see and feel about the issue.

2 What you have to achieve; what you would like to achieve; what work will be needed afterwards.

3 Anticipating reactions. Plan appropriate, unemotional responses.

4 Fall-back position. Helen's fall-back position was to express dissatisfaction and ask for a second interview the next day, when she knew she would feel calmer. Not a bad move, but faced with Joyce's attempt to confuse the issue, Helen would have done well to counter it with a question designed to define the facts.

"I see. You are telling me that you were not having sex?"

In such situations, the manager needs to have a pen poised to record the exact words given in response. This sends the clear message: *You may wish to confuse the issue, but regardless of what has gone before, the facts will be beyond dispute from now on.*

This often has the effect of making the offender play straight.

NEGOTIATIONS

> The more I practise, the luckier I get
> Gary Player

Betty's success in clinching the Thompson deal (*see case study 10*) was followed by an even larger order from the Thompson Group. It was a relatively complicated deal with implications for Vulcan's medium-term financial security. Betty was not particularly interested in crossing t's and dotting i's, as she called it, so she called in Alan to front the negotiations.

George Thompson had a reputation for driving a hard bargain and Alan was wary about dealing with such a tough operator. He made sure that Betty gave him as much advance information about the deal as possible.

When he finally met George Thompson at his office, Alan said: "Look, let's keep this simple. I have a price in mind and so have you. We also have an established relationship. So let's not get embroiled in a war of attrition which ends up with neither of us feeling good.

"If we play games, they'll drag on for weeks, and I don't think that will suit you any more than me. Here's our offer. We'll sell you the computers at the same price as last time for the new order of 20,000. Let's also agree that the price will be higher next time, depending on the size of the order. How does that sound?"

George Thompson was quite impressed by this pragmatic approach. It took them another two hours to sort out the details, including specifications, delivery dates and payment terms. Then they went out to lunch, Alan insisting on paying the bill.

*T*HEORY

Negotiations tend to be a sequence of steps in which both sides gradually surrender ground. They move from their ideal goals towards realistic positions, while trying to ensure that at least they achieve their minimum requirements.

The foundation of good negotiation is assessing the other side's position. This means not only intelligent guesswork as to the best price they can pay, but consideration of what else is in their shopping bag. Alan and Betty already knew that the best price Thompson could pay was the existing price – that agreed for the first order. So the rest of the negotiations depended, rightly, on payment terms, delivery and service, and intangibles such as whether Thompsons enjoyed dealing with Vulcan. They set up the negotiating situation clearly and deftly by reducing the supposedly hot issue of price to just one component of a package.

Alan knew that good negotiators not only think in terms of packages, but that both sides must feel that they have not been beaten into the ground. If they do, they will harbour resentment, and toughen their position for next time.

One other key general point about negotiating: try to give away something which costs you nothing but which is valued by the other side. In this case, it was the apparently minor consideration of the lunch bill. George Thompson was particularly impressed by this gesture because it was something Duncan Johnson had never done.

But always beware that even when bargaining is over, the sharks can still bite. Some seasoned negotiators will try to slip in a last condition at this stage, gambling that your resistance will be low; that you will not want to jeopardise the whole agreement over one last detail.

On to these essential general rules, you also need to graft some specific techniques.

1 ▶ Not only preparation, but **allowing time** for the negotiations is essential for success. The other side may try to wear you down by a series of adjournments timed, tantalizingly, to coincide with points where you seem to be about to reach an important agreement. Both sides should plan enough time to use, and to resist, this technique. It is extravagant on time. Depending on the circumstances, adjournments can use up weeks, even months.

2 ▶ Look for, and talk openly about, **common ground**. Don't concentrate on areas of conflict – give more attention to anticipated common ground. If Alan had been looking for trouble, he might well have found it. As it was, he looked for common ground, and found it quickly.

3 ▶ Identify your, and the other side's, **ideal and realistic settlements**. Discuss them with colleagues. Identify the likely range within which the outcome will fall.

4 ▶ Focus on **issue planning** and avoid **sequence planning**. Don't think in terms of tackling A, then B, then C, then D, in sequence. Plan to consider issue C, for example, as if issues A, B and D don't exist. Remember, your sequence of issues will not be the same as your opposite number's, so be ready to let her behave in the same way.

Here is a typical sequence plan used by average negotiators:

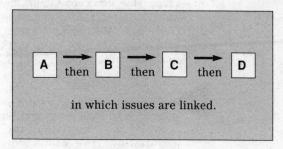

in which issues are linked.

A typical issue plan used by skilled negotiators might be:

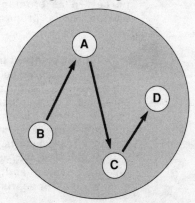

in which issues are independent
and not linked by a sequence.

The clear advantage of issue planning over sequence planning is flexibility. Unless a pre-set agenda has been agreed, which is highly unlikely, the sequence of issues may be subject to negotiation.

5 ▶ **Don't be irritating.** If Alan had said "I'll make you a generous offer", or "I'm perfectly reasonable, don't you think?", he would probably have irritated George Thompson. The words imply that if the other party disagrees, they don't understand the meaning of the concepts of fairness and reason.

6 ▶ **Avoid immediate counter-proposals.** They introduce additional options, sometimes whole new issues, which cloud the clarity of the negotiation. The other side may well be unreceptive because they are still concerned with their initial proposal. And they may also be perceived as blocking manoeuvres or red herrings, not as proposals.

7 ▶ **Don't get involved in a spiral of defence or attack.** Negotiations do involve conflict, but only unprofessional negotiators become heated and emotional. Once one side attacks, the other tends to defend itself automatically; the exchanges become more and more heated, and the downward spiral starts.

If you must attack, and sometimes you must, give no warning, and attack hard. Often the element of surprise will prevent a spiral.

8 ▶ **Give indicators** of how you are going to behave. Instead of asking: "How much will it cost per unit?", warn that you are going to ask a question: "Can we talk about the price now?" Instead of making a specific proposal, say "If I could make a suggestion..." This technique reduces ambiguity and makes the negotiator's intentions clear; it slows the negotiations down, giving time for the talker to gather thoughts and for the other side to clear his or her mind. Indicators also introduce a structure which helps to keep the negotiation on a rational level.

However, it is essential to avoid labelling disagreement. Never say: "I disagree with that because of..." Instead, begin your response by outlining the reasons that lead up to the disagreement.

9 ▶ Sort out misunderstandings by **testing understanding** and **summarizing.** With slippery negotiators, you may need to summarize in writing points already agreed.

10 ▶ Use the **trial close.** "Your pen or mine to sign the deal?" is the classic life policy salesperson's trial close, delivered as soon as they have finished describing their wares. They do not believe for a moment that the customer will buy then and there; they do it as a humorous way to test the water. The customer's response will not result in a sale, but it will probably indicate how far away he or she is from buying.

There comes a point in every negotiation where the sides must actually **close.** The simple, most often-neglected point about closing is that the seller must ask for what she or he wants. Surveys show that the most succesful salespeople are the ones who simply ask more often. Naturally, they choose the right moment to ask, but often enough, the way to conclude (or indeed to start) a negotiation successfully is to **ask for what you want.**

Exercise

If you have been involved in negotiations before, ask yourself:

1 Did I get over-excited or emotional at any stage?

2 Did I have a clear objective?

3 Did I prepare properly?

4 Did I listen to the other party?

5 Did I seek clarification whenever necessary?

6 Did I summarize both positions at every important juncture?

7 What were the circumstances when I eventually made my proposal?

8 Did I look at the entire package? Were there items which I should have included or omitted?

9 Did anyone try to 'slip in' a last-minute item?

10 Did both sides feel entirely satisfied when the negotiations had been concluded?

ORGANIZING A SUCCESSFUL MEETING

A manager is like a football coach. He needs to be smart enough to understand the rules but dumb enough to think the game is important
Eugene McCarthy, U.S. Presidential candidate

Stuart later described his first major crisis at Vulcan as the "worst forty-eight hours of my life".

It began when he heard that Thompsons were having trouble paying a major instalment due to Vulcan on the second major sale contract negotiated by Betty since Stuart's arrival. (*See case study 11*). In his position, how would you set about informing the senior management team of the crisis?

The challenge of this case study is not to dream up the financial package that might save Vulcan. It is to learn how, in a similar crisis, you would set about communicating the issues arising, and ensure that the appropriate lessons are learnt. (The fate of Vulcan will be revealed in a later case study – so be patient.)

Stuart immediately called a meeting with Betty and Alan. His main purpose was to remind them that he should have been consulted about the details of the Thompson order. He proceeded to lay down strict procedural guidelines for the future and entered these new rules in the formal minutes of the meeting.

He had just resolved this issue of control when the phone rang. It was Vulcan's bank, who informed Stuart that Thompsons had now filed for bankruptcy.

Stuart called a full board meeting to tell his managers that Vulcan faced financial disaster. The meeting only lasted five minutes. It was a terse affair. Stuart made it plain he did not want to discuss anything in detail at this stage. "I've just called you here so that I can inform you personally. I didn't want you to find out on the grapevine."

He then held an 'inner war cabinet' with his financial managers, Alan and Matthew, and two bank representatives. Between them they thrashed out several ideas. By the early hours of the following morning they had come up with a rescue package which might keep the company afloat.

The fourth and final meeting involved the whole Vulcan board. If the plan was to be implemented it would mean a major restructuring of the company, including cut-backs in investment. Stuart needed everyone's support. At this point, the blood-letting began.

Betty was furious. "Alan and I spent ages setting up this deal. OK, I admit that we should have brought Stuart into this earlier. But Matthew and Reg Owen are supposed to be in charge of credit control. It's their job to monitor customers' creditworthiness on a continuous basis and tie up doubtful cases like Thompson with letters of credit. Why didn't it happen?"

She then broadened her attack to take in the rest of her colleagues. Matthew was too inexperienced for his level of responsibility. It was Stuart's fault for appointing Matthew in the first place. It was Alan's fault for not controlling Matthew. Campbell was too pedantic and didn't know what was going on. Helen was no help in a crisis...

Eventually Stuart managed to calm her down.

"The sole purpose of this meeting is to agree the new package we have drafted with the banks. I want you to be aware of its implications. We are in for a very rough ride for the next six months and none of us is going to be spared. This is all that needs to be said at this stage.

"Agreed?"

Everyone looked at Betty. Eventually she said "Yes". But it was a reluctant assent and the look she gave Matthew left Stuart a worried man.

THEORY

Stuart had managed to keep his head during this crisis and held four different formal meetings which had four distinct purposes:

1 ▶ **To demonstrate control:** The whole ritualistic mechanism of the formal meeting – agenda, a chairperson with particular privileges, standing orders, minutes, time constraints, seating arrangements – can all be used as mechanisms to demonstrate who is in charge. That is what Stuart did when he called in Alan and Betty and laid down the law about future guidelines.

2 ▶ **To communicate information** to relevant colleagues. It might seem a heavy-handed way to pass on information – usually a memo would suffice – but the meeting has the added advantage that it can encourage instant feedback. In this case Stuart wanted to stop the rumour machine from going into overdrive. His colleagues had to know that the problems were deteriorating and he wanted to tell them himself directly.

3 ▶**To solve problems:** The free exchange of complex ideas was essential. In this case the composition of the meeting was confined to financial experts who could dissect a complicated technical problem. If Betty had been present, it is unlikely they would have been able to concentrate on mere logistics. By carefully choosing this format Stuart was able to hold a constructive meeting which eventually came up with a formula for survival.

4 ▶**Decision-making:** The whole team had to be involved at this meeting as they would be committed to the implementation of any decisions. Stuart had to have the immediate backing of the board to provide a united front to the bank and the rest of the Vulcan staff. Once Stuart had the board's full approval he could begin the restructuring of the company.

By setting up four different kinds of meeting, Stuart had prevented the Vulcan management team from degenerating into a 'talking shop'. Betty, in her outburst, had done just this, but Stuart handled the situation so that she was isolated.

Before every meeting Stuart had asked himself these four questions:

1 Why am I holding this meeting?

2 Why am I taking part?

3 What do I want to achieve at the meeting?

4 What do I want to achieve after the meeting?

To help prepare his objectives, Stuart ensured that the agenda was correct, that all the participants needed to be present and that he had enough allies if needed.

Most managers complain that they have to attend too many meetings: a legitimate grievance. It is usually more practical to communicate in other ways. For instance:

● By meeting people on an individual basis, one-to-one.

● By informal meetings.

● By telephone or fax.

● By writing directly to an individual.

● By issuing a memo to several people.

But the formal meeting is still a useful mechanism. If used properly, it provides a backbone for group communication.

● The chosen audience get, as far as is humanly possible, the same message at the same time.

● Feedback and clarification is possible.

● The message can be restricted in circulation and put in a relevant context.

● Practical and unconsidered information can be included, especially in problem-solving meetings.

● The outcome can be modified in the light of helpful reactions.

EXERCISE

Think of a meeting you have attended recently where there had to be one or all of the following:

- Control

- Communication

- Problem–solving

- Decision–making

Were you aware, before the meeting, which of these aims was intended? Did this awareness improve your contribution to the meeting?

Rate the efficiency of the meeting on a scale of one to ten. Should other methods of communication have been used?

Could you have done without the meeting? If so, how?

LEADERSHIP

DEFINING CORE ELEMENTS

The nail that stands up is the nail that will be hammered down

From the *bushido*, the samurai code of ethics.

"Will you tell me, please, which way I ought to go from here?"
"That depends a good deal on where you want to get to,"
said the cat.
"I don't much care where," said Alice.
"Then it doesn't matter which way you go," said the cat.

Lewis Carroll

Alan's first attempt to help Stuart had backfired. He knew he should have consulted his boss when he became embroiled in the Thompson deal (*case study 12*). Stuart's reaction had been swift.

At the board meeting, described in *case study 13*, he had told Alan in no uncertain terms that he had exceeded his authority and in future he should consult Stuart when such a large contract was being negotiated. The silence from the others gave him a clue that he had hit Alan a little hard. So he had softened the blow:

"Look Alan, I'm pleased that you showed initiative, but really, this is my area of operation. At the very least you should have consulted me first: such a large contract involves strategic thinking, and that's my job, not yours."

Alan had mumbled his apologies and left the boardroom as soon as he could. Once he had got his wits together, he was able to work out what had gone wrong.

Where do you think Alan had gone wrong?

> Should he have stood up to Stuart? After all, Alan was Vulcan's finance director. Did that not mean helping to negotiate payment terms for major contracts?

Verdict No. Alan had quite simply trespassed outside his core job.

What is a core job?

The activity you are paid to do by your company. It is all too easy to refine and evolve a job until it fits you exactly – and ceases to be what you were hired for. Betty, in *case study 5*, was shown to have evolved her job to suit her own valued skills. However, she had at least confined her 'job evolution' to her own area. Even so, she managed to annoy Campbell. Alan had evolved his job outside his area of responsibility. Now he needed to re-evaluate his entire approach to his job, a painful process often triggered only by a crisis. Alan needs to ask: "What am I doing and what should I be doing?"

How would you define Alan's core job as finance director under Stuart? This is the question which Alan put to himself. His honest answer was:

To provide the executive with the best available financial data to ensure that decisions are based on correct information.

Then Alan asked himself: "What would I like my core job to be?" His response to his own question was:

To control Vulcan's long-term financial planning and to become actively involved in preparing the company's strategy.

His core job had been simpler in the past. Duncan Johnson looked upon Alan as a useful clean-up man who would mop up the financial chaos his style of decision-making left behind. Now, Alan was being judged by a new boss, Stuart, who wanted something entirely different. Alan had to adjust accordingly.

*T*HEORY

Understand the objectives of your organization and translate them into your own area of responsibility; then you can start doing your core job. To keep doing it, you must work in terms of standards and targets.

● **Standards:** The minimum requirements of the job.

● **Targets:** Practical, day-to-day working goals which will maintain, indeed improve upon the standards.

The standards by which Alan is judged include:

– Providing Stuart and the bank with accurate monthly reports.
– Keeping a tight control on cash flow.
– Reducing bad debts.
– Complying with the demands of the tax authorities.

Failure to fulfill any of these would put Alan in serious trouble. Alan is paid to do these things, and if he doesn't, someone else will.

Alan's targets, which need to be negotiated with Stuart, are two-fold:

● To support Stuart in the restructuring of the company (and at the same time to secure his own personal future).

● To get into a position where he might help Stuart in the corporate planning process.

Matthew's arrival had, at first, threatened Alan, but after a while he had the idea that he might delegate more and more of the mundane work to Matthew, thereby freeing himself to become involved in the far more interesting area of strategic decision-making.

But he must attain the standards he has set before he can reach the target. For instance, he has to ensure that credit control is tightened up, even if he has delegated it to Matthew.

Job design and job description

Managers, especially new managers, or others like Alan who must work under changed circumstances, can be forgiven for misunderstanding their core jobs because their job descriptions are usually of little help to them. The label usually represents what has already been done in the job. What needs to be done to promote future success always exceeds what has been done in the past.

There is no formula that will guarantee the right job design for an individual. However, there are seven common mistakes, which, if avoided, make it easier for a manager to grow into a job.

1 ▶*Not stretching the manager* The job is so small that the potentially good manager cannot grow. Out of every ten people on a given organizational level, no more than two or three can normally expect promotion. The rest are likely to stay where they are. They need to be given space in which to grow, or they will suffocate.

2 ▶*The non-job* The job must have a specific purpose. A manager must be able to make a contribution that can be identified. The manager must also be accountable.

3 ▶ *Being a working boss* Managing is work, but it is not in itself full-time work. The way to design a managerial job is to balance 'managing' with 'working'. The common complaint that managers don't delegate may well imply that there is an imbalance and that they are taking on the jobs that subordinates should be doing.

4 ▶ *The one-person job* As far as possible a job should be designed so that it can be done by one person working alone, plus the necessary assistants. It is a mistake to design a job so that it requires continuous meetings, co-operation and co-ordination.

5 ▶ *Job titles as rewards:* for example 'Sales Executive' for representative. Job titles create expectations, so to use them as empty substitutes for rank and responsibility is asking for trouble. Change the title only when the function, position or responsibility changes.

6 ▶ *The past-incumbent job* Some jobs manage to defeat one good manager after another. They were often created for an individual who, at some time in the past, had special skills or importance to the organization. What may appear to an outsider as a real job is an accident of personality.

7 ▶ *The old job Things change.* Alan's case is extreme: he had not really changed his attitude to his job as he should have done when Stuart took over from Duncan. No job stays the same.

We all need to review, on a regular basis, whether our core job is redundant, and whether we wish to wait until we are told.

*E*XERCISE

Take a few minutes to analyse your own core job and write it down in the box below, using no more than 25 words.

....
....
....
....
....
....
....
....

Do you think that others will agree with your analysis? Tick the appropriate box:

	yes	no
Your boss	☐	☐
Your colleagues	☐	☐
Your subordinates	☐	☐

If there is some potential conflict, how can you resolve it? Now write down what you would like your core job to become. Is it achievable? Now start working out how you are going to reach your target.

DELEGATING WELL

> One thing delegation is not: an escape from work
> Roger Black, *Getting Things Done*

The Joyce Barber affair (*case study 11*) made Helen realize that she needed to overhaul Vulcan's company disciplinary procedures and bring them up to date. She started to re-write the disciplinary manual, but was not amused when Betty mockingly called it Helen's Problem Page.

Helen did not have a great sense of humour, but she did have a sense of urgency. She realized that her department, Personnel, needed a complete review. She began to write a 'needs analysis' with a gusto which was the envy of her colleagues, including Betty. She devised a new appraisal system, went on two courses, and set about tying up all the loose ends of Vulcan's recruitment and promotional procedures. It was a massive task, but she thrived on the challenge, working 14 hours a day until her husband began complaining about how little time she was spending at home.

Helen had to admit that she could not go on like this. What should she do?

Option 1

> She could abandon her pet projects and concentrate on the basic job for which she had been hired.

Verdict This would not appeal to her at all.

Option 2

> List her current jobs against priorities giving core jobs (case study 14) maximum ratings. Then plan her days accordingly so that she could leave the office at a set time acceptable to her family.

Verdict A time management procedure would be a great help, but there would be a great danger of the non-core work – her pet projects – getting lost.

Option 3

> She could delegate some of the work, say the rewriting of the disciplinary manual.

Verdict In practice it is very difficult to delegate this sort of package to a junior. The effort of briefing would probably be greater than doing the work herself. Creative effort is very personal and the objectives change with every new bit of information and thinking.

Option 4

> Delegate those jobs in her department which had become procedures. The disciplinary manual she could keep to herself.

Verdict This is what Helen did. The result was a short-term loss of efficiency in the department which sorely tried Helen's patience. She found she spent much more time than she liked in briefing her juniors, and overall her job became much more of a worry. She had constantly to remember to monitor people's progress. But this was counterbalanced by increased satisfaction in her own job. She completed the new manual, and her other targets. She also discovered her staff becoming more cheerful and co-operative as time went by.

The skill in delegation is choosing the right things to give to the right people. After that it is a standard management problem.

*T*HEORY

There are four key points to consider when delegating:

1 *Delegation may sound fine in theory but feels bad in practice.*

You cannot delegate well unless you feel secure: if you are afraid for your job, you can hardly donate bits of it to others. It is equally true that you are failing to achieve a major part of a manager's job if you do not delegate.

This is the basic problem with delegating. Points 2, 3 and 4 below analyse it in detail.

2 *Select the right tasks to delegate.*

In theory there ought to be routine bits of work which others can do as well as yourself; but just because they are routine, they still have to be done properly, and delegating them creates the risk that they will be bungled. To offset this risk, work out whether there will be a worthwhile pay-off.

● Will it eventually ease your workload?

● Will it give an assistant useful experience?

● Could it be used to put a questionable employee to the test?

● Might it spread the workload throughout your department?

● How much profit is there in the extra time available to you?

3 ▶*Select the right delegate.*
There is no golden rule: use your instinct; then find the time to monitor and review the employee's performance. "Come and talk to me the day after tomorrow to tell me how it's going," or "I'll ring you every Monday morning between nine and ten to find out how you're doing."

4 ▶*Retain control.*
Delegation does not mean abdication. You retain responsibility and must keep control, but without stifling any initiative which your subordinate might need to show. That is why regular reporting, as suggested in 3, is better than constant monitoring. The easiest trick of maintaining control in a changing world is to retain something that makes you personally indispensable – it could be a detail, or an overview.

Briefing the delegate for the task takes time, but this should be nothing compared to the time saved. Once delegated, the task does not go away; it becomes instead a source of anxiety. One definition of a natural manager is someone who can cope with that anxiety, and at the same time enjoy the rewards of being freed for more challenging, profitable and strategic tasks.

*E*XERCISE

Consider these statements. If you make these kinds of remarks at work, please put a tick in the 'Yes' box. If you don't, tick the 'No' box.

1 If I want something done properly I have to do it myself. Yes ☐ No ☐

2 It's quicker for me to do it myself – showing subordinates takes too much time. Yes ☐ No ☐

3 I've been let down by subordinates too often in the past. Yes ☐ No ☐

4 I'm worried about giving too much power away. I like to feel in control. Yes ☐ No ☐

5 My people simply have not got the expertise/experience which allows me to delegate to them. Yes ☐ No ☐

6 If I do give subordinates a particular job I'm forced to spend too much time supervising them anyway. Yes ☐ No ☐

7 Nobody delegated to me when I was in a junior position. Yes ☐ No ☐

8 If they mess it up, I'll get the blame. Yes ☐ No ☐

9 I enjoy doing the job – and I would miss it if I delegated more. Yes ☐ No ☐

10 I like to spend long hours in the office, doing the extra work. Yes ☐ No ☐

As you have seen in this section, most people are, by nature, poor delegators. If you have answered 'Yes' to six or more of these questions, you need to try harder.

PEOPLE NEED PEOPLE

Hello, I love you, can you tell me your name?
The Doors

"Campbell's cabal is controlling our lives again", muttered Jim Smith angrily as he clocked off. It was true. Every time Campbell was faced with a crisis, he called in his 'A-Team'.

The A-team consisted of three trusted lieutenants, Joe Riley, Don Partridge and Mike Coombes. They were all experienced men on whom Campbell could rely. But Campbell seemed unable to listen to anyone else.

The current crisis was over some faulty supplies which had escaped quality control. The A-team were rushing about trying to test every computer under assembly in order to detect which had been fitted with faulty parts. What galled Jim was that he had known the answer all along. The supplies were part of a consignment which had been delivered during the Easter holidays which had slipped through the system. The problem was therefore confined to a specific part of the assembly line.

At first, Jim enjoyed seeing the A-team scurrying around the factory trying to solve the 'problem'. Eventually his common sense and loyalty got the better of him and he told Campbell the answer, adding: "The trouble with you,

Campbell, is that ninety per cent of the time you're a good manager. But when you have a crisis you drop the rest of us like a ton of bricks. It gets my back up. You don't bother to ask me, so I don't tell you. Simple."

Campbell knew that Jim had a point, but he was furious that one of his workers had held back essential information. He reported Joe Smith to Helen, asking for his file to be marked with a note of the incident. Helen obliged. She also remarked to Campbell that Smith had a right to be noticed. Campbell retorted:

"'Hello Dolly', you mean? Being nice to everybody all the time? Sorry, that's not my style. I *tell* them."

"Telling them is fine provided it's just, related to the job and immediate. Most of us appreciate being treated like adults and told when we have got it wrong."

"I'm not heavy on the praise, they're paid to come here. It's a job."

"Fine, and your staff know that's the way you are. But it wasn't praise or blame Jim was talking about, it was forgetting that he existed. I bet he'd rather you insulted him or were just plain rude. What he can't stand is simply being ignored."

Campbell could not understand what she was on about.

"Where are you going now?" asked Helen.

"To give Jim a blasting for not telling me earlier – do you think he'll enjoy that?"

Helen sighed.

> You probably agree with Helen; but what precisely can be done to improve Campbell's style? He cannot change his personality overnight. This is a deep-rooted problem. So what are the options?
>
> ● Go on a course?
>
> ● Talk the matter over in depth with his A-Team?

● Talk it over with Jim and the rest of the staff?

● Make strenuous efforts to include Jim Smith and others next time there is a crisis?

● Widen the membership of the A-team to include Jim and a few more trustworthy people?

The last two options are of course the best, but they are unattainable. Campbell is entrenched in his position, and so is his A-Team. There is little point in radically changing his style to please the Jim Smiths if at the same time he only upsets his valued henchmen in the A-Team. What Campbell needs to do is find a **balance** which enables him to act more appropriately when under pressure.

THEORY

People need people.

As a boy, Campbell's most heady experience of praise from his strict father would have been: "You did well." Campbell still remembers the day he qualified with a first-class honours in production engineering. His father actually touched his shoulder – without, of course, catching his eye. You had to do something in the Ritchie household in order to gain recognition. Helen's home was entirely different. She, her twin sister and her mother were very close, indeed demonstrative in their shows of affection. The two styles are, in fact, perfectly viable, provided they are used in appropriate situations, and don't get out of hand.

Campbell's style is, A-team apart, appropriate to the production department. Up to a point, people respect him for it because at least it is sincere. They could sense that they had done something well simply by the way he walked past their bench, and most of the skilled and semi-skilled workers preferred this sparse, 'masculine' approach, except on days when they were completely ignored.

Stuart, on the other hand, was perfectly at home in Helen's department and was always pleased to be asked to their get-togethers.

It is a manager's duty not only to give recognition, but to work out the amount and the type of recognition appropriate to his field.

EXERCISE

Think of occasions when you have deprived colleagues of simple, social recognition. Then reflect on how much recognition you need. Compare the two. Attempt to analyse the contrasting values in detail.

Give brief written answers to the questions below, plus a rating on a scale of zero to ten. One means never; ten means very frequently.

How often do you give recognition to others for doing well?	How often do you accept the praise of others?
....	....
....	....
....	....
....	....
....	....
Rating	Rating

How often do you ask others for praise?	How often do you avoid praising others?
....	....
....	....
....	....
....	....
....	....
Rating	Rating

Campbell's completed questionnaire would look like this:

How often do you give recognition to others who do well?

When they do better — beyond their job.

Rating [2]

How often do you accept the praise of others?

Honestly it worries me. I feel it's not true.

Rating [2]

How often do you ask others for praise?

Never.

Rating [2]

How often do you avoid praising others?

Very often if they are paid to do a job. why praise them for it?

Rating [2]

Analysis

Anything below five points means the level of recognition and praise could be improved. But at least, in Campbell's case, the balance is there: he does not want more than he gives and as a result he will be respected, at least by some, for his integrity.

If the numerical ratings for your questionnaire are out of balance by more than three points, you need to work on this problem.

INFLUENCING SKILLS

> The shortest and best way to make your fortune is to let people
> see clearly that it is in their interests to promote yours
>
> La Bruyère, *Characters*, 1688

Matthew knew that Stuart was disappointed with his progress.
He had been the first manager Stuart had appointed
personally at Vulcan. His brief had been clear enough – to
modernize the accounts department – and he had gone far
towards achieving this. He had also earned admiration for the
way he handled disgruntled subordinate Reg Owen (*case
study 3*). He was no longer the somewhat retiring new
recruit; indeed he seemed to have found a self-confidence
which the rest of the team felt was unwarranted. Some were
calling him pushy. In fact, the glitter was now falling off him
at an alarming rate. He and Reg Owen had taken most of
the blame for the Thompson fiasco (*case study 13*) which
even now still threatened to bring Vulcan to its knees.

Each of the senior managers was aware, every working

day, that the affair threatened all of their futures. The discipline of working within the new financing package was a constant irritation. These frustrations seemed to be expressing themselves as a generally cynical attitude towards Matthew: Matthew was, in fact, a scapegoat.

When Matthew was not being overworked by the complications of refinancing Vulcan, he could dwell unhappily on the fact that Alan had craftily distanced himself from the Thompson débâcle. One day he overheard Stuart say: "Alan is not quite the old-timer I thought he was. He's got vision and experience. I think we're going to need him if we're to survive this mess." Matthew's spirits sank even further.

Matthew needed to consider his position. What should he do?

Option one | Should he look for another job?

Verdict He could not give in after one setback. This would not be a smart career move. After all, Vulcan was his first major job. He must avoid another failure so soon after the unfortunate outcome of his university career (*case study 1*).

Option two | Regain the initiative with some conspicuous success?

Verdict Matthew will, in fact, attempt to regain the initiative with what proves to be a high-risk strategy (*see case study 29*). The very process of looking for something sensational and impressive will deflect him from his core job (*see case study 14*).

Option three

> Extend his sphere of influence. Look for allies who would say the right things about his work to the right people.

Verdict

Another option worth considering. Unfortunately Matthew is not a political animal and this approach would not come naturally to him. Anyway, who would be his allies?

Option four

> Ignore the implied criticism and pretend nothing has happened?

Verdict

When an ambitious newcomer's star is in decline, everyone knows it. Matthew could ignore the fact, but others would not. Their manner towards Matthew has changed; he cannot do anything about it.

Option five

> Adopt a low profile and regroup.

Verdict

This would be quite sensible. Matthew is good at his job and should not become too despondent after one setback. By accepting the challenge, in a peaceful spirit, he could regain the initiative – but it would take time.

All of these viable options were worth considering, and Matthew tried a number of them. Here, we will follow option three: extending his sphere of influence.

He decided, wisely, that this should not be a personal campaign but should be based on the larger issue of modernising the accounts department.

THEORY

First, a 'health warning'. Influencing is a polite word for manipulation, and, as we have said, Matthew is not good at company politics. His attempts to influence, as you will discover, are doomed to failure. You, the reader, may or may not be better suited to the political game.

Every leader needs a power-base – and to achieve this he or she must master the art of influencing others. In order to devote the effort to the right people, you need to divide your colleagues into different classes: those who have power, and those who are cause for concern.

Power Don't confuse power with job title. Some people enjoy far more power than their position in the organization would otherwise suggest. They are, typically, in a sensitive post that gives them inside knowledge. Anne Dudley enjoyed considerable power when she was Duncan Johnson's private secretary. Now that she is in Campbell's office, her importance has waned.

Concern People who have a vested interest in something, or somebody, are a matter for concern, even if they have no power. Reg Owen might not have much power, but he has become Matthew's ally and will do all he can to help his new boss. Concern can be negative as well as positive. At first, Reg's concern was anti-Matthew (*case study 3*).

The point of looking at your colleagues in these two ways is that it will make you direct your efforts at appropriate groups or 'clusters'. You don't want to market yourself in the manner of a peak-time TV commercial – appealing to anyone and everyone. That would be too inaccurate. Nor do you want to go to the opposite extreme, and market yourself to each individual customer. That would be too blatant. The happy compromise is deliberately to disclose appealing information about yourself to appropriate clusters.

In Matthew's case, there were five clusters of people who needed to be treated in different ways in order to extend his sphere of influence.

1 ▸ Those already in the circle of influence

Those already on your side are an area of continuous concern, and to ignore them (as Campbell found out in *case study 16*) is fatal.

ACTION Keep them in the picture about your ideas and plans. Don't antagonise them in your efforts to gain wider acceptance.

2 ▸ High power/high concern individuals or groups

These have a large investment in whether you succeed or fail – and have relevant power. Of course, you have to know who they are, and how to treat them appropriately.

Stuart comes into this category. He is concerned in Matthew's success and has the power to influence the outcome.

Vulcan's bank is a true high power/high concern group for Matthew. The manager and his staff know that Matthew's performance could have a crucial bearing on the future of Vulcan.

Stuart and the bank need to hear much the same sort of information from Matthew, presented in broadly similar ways. The bank manager would probably respond well if Matthew were to ask 'Do you find the way I'm presenting the financial data helpful?' Stuart needs to be made aware that Matthew wants the accounts department to shape up to Stuart's liking. 'Is this how you see it? How often do you want a detailed progress report? I could speed it up if...'

Matthew needs to reflect on who else comes into this category. Does Alan? Matthew makes a serious mistake in not realizing that his immediate boss has the potential to be high power/high concern.

3 ▶ High power/low concern

Matthew thinks that Alan falls into this group: he has power, but he feels threatened by Matthew and does not have a vested interest in his success. How to treat him? Matthew should recognize that Alan's power-base is too strong now to be eroded by others comparing his achievements with Matthew's. He should not try to impress, or to alienate, Alan or Alan's admirers. He should never publicly contradict him, or challenge him, as he has done before. He should stay neutral, avoid grovelling, and exhibit patience: time, at least in theory, is on Matthew's side rather than Alan's. Matthew should stop looking like a young man in a hurry and start looking like one who has the patience, and professionalism, to wait until he can replace Alan. Others will then find Matthew a less risky cause to support than at present.

4 ▶ Low power/high concern

Like voters, they are not powerful individually, but they are concerned in Matthew's fate and could be organized to present a unified voice on Matthew's behalf.

Reg Owen is one of them: he has now befriended Matthew and will do everything in his power to help his new boss. Unfortunately, Reg has little power but at least he will ensure that Matthew's back is protected in the accounts department. They don't require active wooing, but they do deserve the courtesy of being kept up to date with developments at Matthew's level.

Matthew should tell Reg once a week as much as is possible about what is happening in the company at a senior level.

5 ▶ *Low influence/low concern*

'Spectators': At best indifferent to Matthew, his problems and his goals. Initially, this group included Campbell, Helen and Betty. They were not much concerned with what they considered to be the detailed analysis of figures, but after the Thompson disaster they are beginning to take an active interest in Matthew, particularly Betty. They are potentially an organized, hostile force.

Matthew has to prepare answers to this group's potential criticisms and have them ready at the first sign of criticism, open or implied.

Matthew wrote a list of his colleagues and assigned them to the various categories:

Stuart: High power/high concern

Alan: High power/low concern

Reg: Low power/high concern

Campbell, Helen and Betty: Low power/low concern

Do you agree with his analysis?

In fact, he made one bad mistake, despite taking the trouble to think it out. He mis-filed Betty.

Her newly displayed hostility (*case study 13*) was the clue he should have picked up on to alert him to her high concern. She was taking an active interest in his work, because she saw that if Matthew failed, her own schemes might suffer. Moreover, she did not have his interests at heart.

EXERCISE

Try analysing your own colleagues at work into clusters as described above. Then define a different way of treating each group that would best serve your interests.

Now single out your closest competitor at work. Do the same analysis for him or her.

How do the groups differ from yours? Often, analysing someone else's potential position helps you see your own with extra objectivity. It may help to pinpoint flaws in the analysis you did for yourself.

If it seems like a formal exercise, it is meant to be. Everyone should approach this area with caution: the whole point of it is to sift the political situation. If Matthew found it easy to make a serious mistake even when he analysed his position formally, imagine how easy it is to make mistakes when leaving it to hunch.

DECISION-MAKING

Knowing the answers means asking the right questions.
Finding the right questions is the art of management
Mike Woods, *The Manager's Casebook*, 1992

"Disaster," said Betty. "Gemstar know all about our bid for Thompson International. Now they've put in one better themselves."

Stuart groaned, dialled Alan's internal number and said: "Alan, we've been beaten by Gemstar. It's back to the starting line I'm afraid."

Alan's idea to take over Thompson International, a division of the now bankrupt Thompson Group, had been brilliant. The bank had said yes immediately because the 'fit' was so perfect. For a rock-bottom price, which could be recouped within six months, Vulcan would be able to close down a break-even area of its own production line, with major cost savings, and replace it with a less costly one, producing a superior type of hardware.

Betty had worked day and night on her overseas contacts, lining up, under wraps, much bigger orders than Thompson had ever been able to find for the product. The increased sales would have cured Vulcan's cash problem within a year.

Very few people at Vulcan knew about the proposal and Betty was convinced that there had been a leak. Two weeks later she got a possible answer. Her number two, Doug Evans, gave in his resignation and told her he was leaving to join rivals Gemstar.

"That pig sold us out," she confided to her dog that evening. Doug had been privy to the bid plan, along with a handful of other senior members of her department.

The Gemstar affair was the biggest crisis (so far) of Betty's working life. Not only was Vulcan's future once more in jeopardy, but she, Betty, was uncomfortably close to the source of the problem. Her fellow directors were saying nothing, but she could tell by their manner that they thought she must have alienated Doug Evans in one of her more excitable moods.

She could not prove that Doug had sabotaged their plans, so she set about trying to find evidence. She was not actually on trial for the débâcle, but she was certainly on probation.

If you were Betty, how would you set about discovering whether a leak had been sprung?

Option one

> To sort it out by making enquiries outside Vulcan, keeping it a secret from her staff. After all, she was not sure whom she could trust. She could not advertise the disappointment felt by Vulcan's senior management at losing the bid, because that would have alerted outsiders to the seriousness of Vulcan's cash problems. These were, for now, confidential to the senior management team.

Verdict

A reasonable gut reaction, but she simply did not have the right leads to deal with such a sensitive matter on her own. Equally, Vulcan's interest in taking over a business such as Thompson International should remain as confidential as possible.

Option two | Share the problem with trusted senior members of her staff and make a decision based on their advice?

`Verdict` This was Betty's usual approach, but it was inappropriate at present. Betty could not be sure that one of her 'confidants' was not in some way to blame.

Option three | To get what information she could from juniors among her staff and then to act accordingly, again by herself.

`Verdict` This was the right short-term answer. She faced a crisis; she needed to know what had happened. She had to be seen to be doing something, and however embarrassing it might be to tell her juniors about the situation, she must pay that price for any information that would establish the facts about Doug and his departure.

THEORY

Good managers draw on a range of decision-making styles. All have their place:

Authoritarian The manager makes a decision without reference to anyone else in his or her organization, as in Option one. Once made, the decision may not be negotiated.

Actually there are two types of authoritarian decision-making: 'A1', in which the boss solves the problem using the information available at the time; and 'A2', where the boss collects the relevant information from subordinates and then decides on a solution.

He or she may or may not choose to tell the subordinates about the nature of the problem while collecting the information. The subordinates act as a data source and are not involved in the decision-making process.

Consultative This is where the manager shares the problems with relevant subordinates and again this can be approached in two ways: 'C1', where the manager consults chosen subordinates on an individual basis and explains that he or she will make a considered decision which may or may not reflect individual advice; and 'C2', where the boss shares the problem with a group of subordinates, explaining that the decision may or may not reflect the suggestions and views collected.

Group The manager shares a problem with a group of subordinates and gives them formal permission to develop alternatives. Once the group has produced a solution or decided on a strategy, the boss will carry out their wishes.

In order to match the most appropriate style of

decision to the circumstances, you have to ask yourself a sequence of simple questions.

1 ▶ Are you, the decision-maker, free to decide? With some decisions, the manager really is the decision-maker – what they say goes; they have full freedom. In others, the manager may look like the decision-maker, but in reality he or she is an agent of some other person or body – the bank, the union, the board.

Betty was, in this case, operating under the cold stare of her board, anything but a free agent. The fact that she is not free also rules out the group decision alternative. If the group decides to let the culprit off with an informal warning, Betty will have failed in her objective to demonstrate to fellow directors that she is innocent – and in control.

2 ▶ Does the manager have enough information to make the decision without speaking to anyone else? In Betty's case, she does not. If Betty did have enough information, she could make an A1 decision. As it is, she has the choice either of becoming a private detective, or of consulting with others.

3 ▶ Do subordinates need to be persuaded that the solution is just? In this case, Betty simply needs to tell the board that Doug did or did not do such-and-such a thing with help from X who has now been fired, and matters will move on. If someone in the department does not like it, too bad for them.

4 ▶ How much power has the decision-maker got? In this case, Betty clearly has enough power to act alone, and act she must. It would be different if she was accusing an existing member of staff, in a department not her own.

5 ► **Will colleagues agree with the decision?**
As Betty makes this decision, she must watch her back. If a person, or a group, is going to disagree with this decision in order to undermine her position, she needs to point at others who do agree with her decision. She needs to canvass support on a private basis before announcing her course of action at the next board meeting.

6 ► **Are there time constraints?** Time can override everything. Consultation takes time. If it is not available, you will have to fall back on an authoritarian style.

*E*XERCISE

Think of a management decision you have been involved with recently.

1 Which decision-making style did you adopt?

2 Think how you could have used another style in each situation, and the consequences if you had done so.

– In practical terms, how could you have implemented the strategy?
– What would have been the immediate consequences?
– What would have been the long-term pay-off for your organization?

3 With hindsight, did you do right?

The Team

STAGES OF
TEAM DEVELOPMENT

> To see what is in front of one's nose needs a constant struggle
> George Orwell

Stuart was in a surprisingly positive mood at the board meeting called to review the collapse of the Thompson International take-over. He began with the words: "Vulcan is going to rise again."

It was not an idle boast: he really believed it. Losing the deal to Gemstar had been a major setback, but there were some positive signs emerging from within Vulcan itself. Betty and Alan were growing in stature, Campbell and Helen were providing solid support, while Matthew was trying his best in their wake. This particular group of managers was beginning to form a team. So far so good, thought Stuart.

But the mood among the others at the board meeting was grim. Betty summed up their feelings: "It's just one disaster after another – Vulcan's jinxed." Stuart had to stop the rot. "Think positive," he boomed, and he proceeded to recount the story of the manic depressive who was having psychiatric treatment.

"'Two months ago I inherited two hundred thousand from my aunt, last month I won a hundred thousand on the pools.'

"'What's wrong?' asked the psychiatrist.

"'This month, nothing.'"

They all laughed. Stuart said: "If we keep our nerve, we'll be able to see this thing through. We might even make money out of it."

"What do you mean?" asked Campbell.

"That's something for the future," said Stuart mysteriously.

They all tried to pin him down but Stuart would not give in. "I'll tell you about it all in good time. Now let's get down to sorting out some new marketing ideas..."

Stuart was beginning to look more to the future. He realized that he and Vulcan were now at 'the end of the beginning'. It was a critical phase which could well define the future survival of the company.

It takes time to develop a group of individuals into a first-class management team: they have to go through a sometimes painful growing process. Look at these four stages below: try to identify which stage Vulcan has now reached. You may also find it helpful to look back at case study 4, where Helen learnt to communicate more easily with Stuart by understanding his needs when it came to communicating with others. The stages of team formation described below are concerned with numbers of individuals establishing their needs from a particular group in a set sequence.

Stage one:

> ## Identification with the group – the undeveloped team

It takes any group of people time to settle down every time they meet. On a daily basis the settling down process at work may be over a cup of coffee where the inconsequential chatter allows individuals to adjust and reaffirm that they are part of the group. With a group of people working together for the first time, the process may take much longer than it takes to drink a cup of coffee. For various reasons, the manager may be impatient and not allow that time.

The management problem with a new group is this: when people first meet, unless they get firm direction and control, the settling down stage may last for ever. You have a social club, not a working unit. The manager needs to allocate, control and monitor, otherwise things do not get done. An authoritarian style of management is essential at this stage.

However, if the manager never relaxes the authoritarian approach, the group cannot settle in and cannot develop into a team. They never think for themselves and they never contribute to the management process: they need everything on a plate. You hear them say:

"When I come into work, I hang my coat and my mind up on the peg – it's the only way to survive round here."

The creative manager allows the individuals in the group time to find out what is expected of them, and the purpose of what they are doing. The group can then move towards being an undeveloped team. It acts something like a group of comparative strangers at a bar. You will hear 'bar talk' – often repeated, vigorous debates on inconsequential matters – and plenty of grumbling. You will also find acceptance of the rules and deference to the 'host' coupled with a reliance on the host actually to organize anything. You also get guarded exchanges of information and one-sided attempts to define positions. There may also be temporary groupings between obviously similar people.

Stuart certainly could not, and therefore did not, allow his group of directors to remain an undeveloped team – he needed them to share the load with him.

Stage two:

> **Understanding roles and developing clarity of purpose – the developing team**

Once the individuals in a group have been encouraged to settle in and understand the overall purpose of their presence, they need to define exactly how they fit in.

Campbell, for instance, observed:

"OK, Vulcan needs to increase cashflow. I can see how marketing contributes – what exactly do you want from production – less inventory?" He had it right, but the consequence was a minor row with Betty when she asked him for some more variations on the standard line of laptop:

"Fine – but that puts up inventory. Come on, let's see Stuart, he can work it out."

Individuals will probe for their status in a group and in some cases may be fearful that unofficial roles allocated by fellow members may not suit them. Matthew, for instance, had seen himself as a progressive ideas person, whereas Betty's easier style and experience is beginning to take over that role in the group. Alan, in his own quiet way, is also eating away on the 'softer' side of finance and accounting and Matthew is being left with the more boring jobs.

Stuart has to ride out this stage, which is by no means over. He will notice:

- Defensiveness, competition and jealousy.

- Challenges to the structure, nature and purpose of the task.

- Experimental hostility and aggressiveness to him and others.

- Testing of roles.

● Intense, brief and brittle links – clique and faction formation and decay.

He will need to be patient, using consultative management styles, with a strong authoritarian style in reserve. Things, as he knows, can only get better, but it is likely that blood will be spilt.

Stage three: | **Establishing trust between individuals – the consolidating team**

The consolidating team has solved a great number of its problems and is establishing an identity with norms of behaviour. The Vulcan team has not reached this stage, and is unlikely to do so in the immediate future. A truly consolidating team is proud of itself and develops its own routine of working. Stuart is aware of this and that was his reason for beginning the board meeting with the encouraging remarks.

What Stuart would like to see is:

● Acceptance of him as part of the team, as well as accepting his special position as chief executive.

● An open exchange of information and problems.

● The expression of feelings and concerns in appropriate ways.

● Constructive criticism and requests for advice and support.

● A reduction in pointless conflict and an establishment of group identity.

The first sign that the Vulcan board was moving into the consolidating stage came quite soon after their latest board meeting when Helen attempted to arrange a drink to celebrate the anniversary of Vulcan's foundation. Matthew opposed the idea on the grounds that it would be too formal. Stuart deduced from this minor episode that the team was not really consolidating yet, and still needed him to settle differences in a semi-authoritarian style.

Stage four:

The mature team

The mature team is self-sufficient and only needs guidance.

When the Vulcan team is truly mature, Stuart will notice:

● Trust and a free interchange of information.

● Everyone simply getting on with the job. The people problems will be handled in a matter-of-fact way, without fuss.

● Clear, understood, negotiated and accepted (but flexible) roles.

The challenge to Stuart is to balance his own role with the new impetus and authority of the team. He needs to retain control of external contacts; he needs to steer the team; he also needs to work with, or possibly in, it.

His final, and perhaps most difficult job, is to recognize that the mature team, although fun to belong to, is inclined to alienate outsiders and to repel new members. Without this critical overview, which is Stuart's responsibility, the mature team can become smug – 'married' to itself. Over time, it could destroy Vulcan.

E XERCISE

Teams can exist and function well in all four stages described above. The stage merely needs to be appropriate to the circumstances.

● Think of circumstances where each stage would be effective.

● Think of your own management team:

– In what stage of development would you put it?

– How do the objectives and behaviours described above fit your team?

● Is the stage of development of your team appropriate to the task the team has to perform?

● If not, what could you do to improve things?

THE NEED TO HAVE BALANCE IN A TEAM

> I resign. I wouldn't want to belong to any club that
> would have me as a member
>
> Groucho Marx

Stuart was beginning to believe that Vulcan might have the
makings of a good management team when he came down to
earth with a bump.

It happened when the team was trying to find ideas to
help Betty improve Vulcan's marketing strategy.

Stuart had given them plenty of advance warning about
the project and was looking forward to discussing their ideas
in detail. But he was bitterly disappointed by the response.

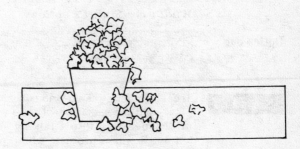

Matthew, who was still trying to make a come-back (*case study 17*), produced a deluge of suggestions; Alan was not far behind. Betty's ideas were fewer, and slightly better-conceived – but they lacked form and she spoilt the meeting by making funny noises whenever Matthew opened his mouth.

"I'm amazed," said Stuart. "Call yourself professional managers? This is just a ragbag of ideas which could have been written on the back of a beer mat. Our survival depends on producing winning ideas.

"Campbell and Helen have got none at all. Some of Alan's aren't bad, but as for Betty and Matthew... Have you never thought that as directors on the same board you should work together?"

Stuart saw the problem starkly. His managers were functioning well in their own particular departments, but there was an overall lack of balance in the team.

● There were too many ideas floating around, and there was no one to distinguish the wood from the trees.

● There was insufficient attention to detail. Alan and Helen were the only people remotely concerned with detail.

What were Stuart's options?

Option one

> Do nothing at all and accept it as a fact of life. After all, no team is perfect.

Verdict

True, but there was now no cohesive marketing plan – and the management team was in danger of degenerating into a talking-shop with no action. It was a problem which could not be ignored.

Option two

> Try to improve some of the individuals by sending them on training courses: report writing for Matthew; assertiveness for Campbell; listening skills for Betty.

Verdict

This is a medium- to long-term solution, with no guarantees.

Option three

> Bring in someone from outside to provide the missing ingredients.

Verdict

Easier said than done. Taking on new staff is not cheap; recruitment and selection is always chancy, and the new person would need time to settle into the team. Not only a long-term solution, but a risky one.

Option four

> Develop someone from within the organization to provide the necessary balance.

Verdict

This is a far more attractive proposal. But whom?

*T*HEORY

Any management team has two dimensions. The first dimension is defined by the task skills required to do the core job: Alan and Matthew need to be good at finance, Campbell needs to be a competent production engineer and Helen needs to know her industrial relations law.

The second dimension is the style in which the managers go about their jobs.

Management style can be summarized in a wheel diagram:

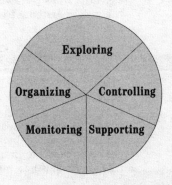

Different people are best in different sectors of the wheel. Both Betty and Matthew value and enjoy the first sector – the exploring part of the management wheel, although they both have valued skills in the controlling sector, too. Ideally, Betty and Matthew like to be on the look-out, spotting new lands to conquer.

Campbell and Stuart are both concerned with

the organizing and the controlling sectors – they like to make things happen, while Alan is happiest monitoring activities. Helen sees herself being most effective in the fifth sector of the management wheel, the supporting sector.

Any effective team needs to have enough task skills actually to complete work in hand. But unless it also has exploring, organizing, controlling, monitoring and supporting skills, in proper balance with each other, it will fail.

These ideas are based on the pioneering work of Meredith Belbin, the distinguished Cambridge management theorist. He believes that the individual's contribution to a team is moulded by personal preference, and identifies nine essential roles for a viable team; and that these roles all contribute to the five key management activities.

Exploring skills

These provide a team with ideas and contacts. The Belbin Roles which contribute to exploring skills are known as the PLANT (PL) and the RESOURCE INVESTIGATOR (RI).

The PL values ideas. Betty is a typical PL; Matthew is not far behind. The RI likes to make contacts, just like Betty. Unfortunately, this is a role which Matthew also enjoys.

Organizing skills

If exploring skills are to be exploited properly by the team they have to be organized by a CO-ORDINATOR (CO) who is the diplomat of the group; also by an IMPLEMENTER (IMP) who is the planner.

The CO values getting people to work together; both Stuart and Helen have this quality. The IMP is concerned with the practicalities of organizing: Betty's and Helen's weakness, but Campbell's and Stuart's strength.

Controlling skills

Organization does not get things done, it only eases the way. To get things done you need controlling skills.

The SHAPER (SH) gets things done by leading from the front. If anything, the Vulcan team has too many shapers: Campbell, Betty and Matthew are all impatient to get down to it and produce visible results.

Monitoring skills

Without monitoring skills, teams often get the wrong things done and often fail to complete tasks. This essential area is looked after by the MONITOR EVALUATOR (ME) and the COMPLETER FINISHER (CF). The ME makes sure that standards are maintained, but can be over-critical: Campbell and Alan have this trait, but not Betty and Matthew. The CF is 'the dotter of i's and crosser of t's', a role all too often left to some underling; but Stuart is lucky – Helen and Alan are very detail-conscious.

Support skills

These are easily lost among more obvious types of management activity, but nonetheless important. The relevant Belbin types are the TEAM WORKER (TW) and the SPECIALISTS (SP).

TWs enjoy warm and friendly work groups and try to establish stable working relationships. Stuart and Campbell, who don't possess the quality themselves, are beginning to welcome it in others and allow Helen, in her unassertive way, to make life more pleasant and the team more effective. Helen, along with Matthew, also practises the last of the Belbin roles, that of SP. Both of them value in-depth knowledge and regret the generalism of general management.

Defined in these terms, Stuart's team has the Belbin profile illustrated below.

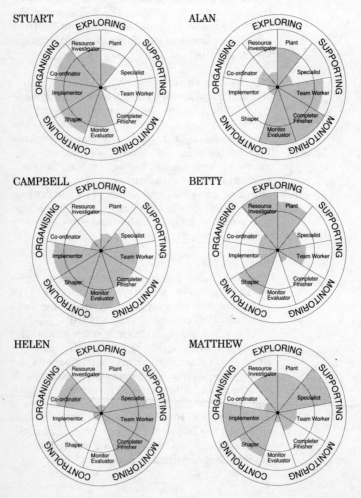

To discover how well your own team is balanced, shade in each
member's relevant segment on one wheel. If one segment is left
unshaded, the team lacks balance. The scoring system described
under **Exercise** on the following pages will assist this process.

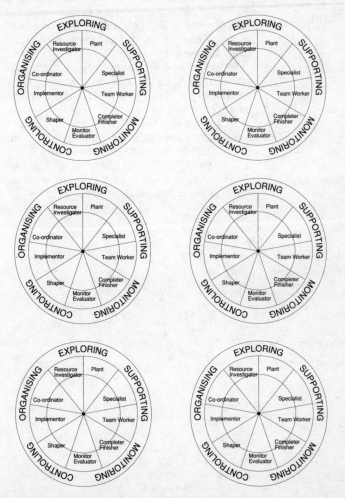

On the whole Stuart is satisfied that he can build a viable team from these components, although Matthew and Betty are perhaps too much alike. Apart from that, the team is surprisingly balanced. Alan and Helen are undoubtedly the stabilising factors and Betty, with or without Matthew, will be out there making waves. Properly used, Campbell, with support from Matthew, has potential.

Belbin's system encourages you to take a structured look at a team's strengths and weaknesses and can help any manager to build a balanced team.

As few as two individuals can supply all the necessary roles to lead a successful team – provided they have adequate back-up.

However, you should guard against applying Belbin's theory too literally. There is no such thing as a perfectly-balanced team.

*E*XERCISE

Which of the five major functions – *Exploring*, *Organizing*, *Controlling*, *Monitoring* and *Supporting* – are you best at?

Then give yourself a score, on a scale of one to eight, for the Belbin roles. Those roles in which you rate yourself between five and eight are likely to be your natural team roles, the ones you enjoy using most. To help with assessing your scores, a chart showing the Vulcan team's is given on the next page.

The roles in which you score between four and two are back-ups, for use when pressed. Plan to improve upon them for when the need arises. For instance, if there were a shortage of CFs in your team and you were reasonably strong in this area, you might develop the role further for the general good.

Roles for which you score one or zero are best forgotten; ensure, instead, that other members of your team can offset this shortage.

If you are not sure about your team role profile, ask a colleague to complete the questionnaire.

If they don't agree with your assessment, ask them why not. Even when your roles have been clearly defined, you should review them from time to time.

● Are they still appropriate for the task your are performing?

● Are there any shortcomings appearing elsewhere in your team?

● What further training and development needs can you identify as a result?

Are the essential management skills described here, and the accompanying Belbin roles, valued in your own team? If not, what should you do about it?

Self Perception Inventory Scores

Firm: Vulcan Computing

Candidate Name	PL	RI	CO	SH	ME	TW	IMP	CF	SP
ALAN	4	1	2	1	8	6	1	8	1
BETTY	7	8	2	7	0	3	1	1	2
CAMPBELL	2	1	1	6	8	4	6	4	3
HELEN	1	1	6	1	0	8	1	8	6
MATTHEW	7	1	2	6	1	2	8	2	8
STUART	3	4	6	6	4	1	6	0	0
TOTAL	24	16	19	27	21	24	23	23	20
AVERAGE	4.00	2.66	3.16	4.50	3.50	4.00	3.83	3.83	3.33

THE PROBLEM OF THE ODD MAN OUT

When one door closes, the next one is inclined to slam in your face

Graffito in a corporate wash-room

Stuart had once thought that Matthew would be an essential member of an improved management team at Vulcan. Now he recognized that he was becoming unproductive.

First, there was the overlap with Alan. There was now nothing that Matthew could do that Alan did not do as well, if not better. Stuart admitted to himself that he had been too hasty in appointing Matthew. He feared that although Alan had resisted Matthew's attempt to take over some of his job, the continued aggravation of his presence ("In other words, his pushiness," mused Stuart) would get to Alan and make him take early retirement.

Now, to make matters worse, Matthew was aggravating Betty. Their team roles seemed to be in conflict (*case study 13*) and Betty was complaining that he was interfering in her department.

Stuart felt sorry for Matthew, but he knew that he could not afford to lose Alan or Betty: if they went, the team would evaporate.

If you were Stuart, how would you make sure Alan was happy enough to stay at Vulcan for the forseeable future?

Option one

Leave well alone and hope that things might work out in the long run?

Answer

It might not be a bad idea. Alan had already shown he could handle a crisis. He could handle long-term aggravation too, if he wanted. But that was a risk Stuart dared not take.

Option two

Defuse the situation by giving Matthew a new responsibility? He had emerged as someone full of ideas. Perhaps Stuart should give him a special brief to help Betty prepare the new marketing plan?

Answer A mistake, and one that Stuart would regret.

Option three Give Alan a special project which would allow him to shine?

Answer Just another empty gesture which could further demotivate Alan. Alan was no fool: he could recognize that Stuart was trying to mollfiy him and would be embarassed by the charade.

Option four Recognize Alan's seniority by giving him an additional title to enhance his prestige?

Answer Same as for option three.

None of these options is good enough. Stuart needed to find out what really motivated Alan. Alan was a mature manager, capable of analysing his predicament in an objective way (*see case study 2*). He would welcome an open exchange of views with Stuart.

During their talk, Alan confided to Stuart that his ambition all along had been to become more closely involved in working out Vulcan's long-term strategy. "Don't worry, I'm not after your job," Alan said. "But I need the stimulus of applying my financial knowledge to the company's long-term development. The day-to-day stuff doesn't satisfy me like it used to."

Stuart quickly agreed that they should share all Vulcan's strategic planning work, meeting regularly, and privately, to discuss future developments.

*T*HEORY

The basic problem was that Stuart had been unsure how to motivate Alan.

The motivation of staff is one of the most complex aspects of management, involving internal and external factors, known and unknown. Stuart's starting point was to look at things from Alan's viewpoint, trying to discover his needs. From there he could try to dovetail them with those of the organization.

It hardly needs saying that if you are to bring out the best in people, you have to understand in depth what is likely to make them tick. One of the most widely accepted guides to what motivates people at work is Maslow's Hierarchy of Needs.

More sophisticated needs

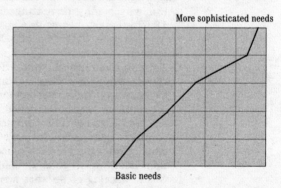

Basic needs

Maslow's key point is that once a need is satisfied, more sophisticated ones will automatically emerge.

Survival needs

In modern society, these usually come down to money: enough money to eat a healthy diet and to pay the home loan. Some people reappraise these basic needs and adopt alternative values, but this does not disprove the existence of the basic need.

Security
Once survival needs are satisfied, people begin to think of the future: they become concerned with job security, health insurance and pension.

Belonging
When security needs are satisfied, thoughts turn to social life: you start wanting to belong to a group.

(Stuart himself needed to belong to a successful team, and was always frustrated by slow progress towards this end. When he had first joined Vulcan, he had told his wife that he would leave if he did not succeed within the first 18 months.)

Esteem
This need includes both self-respect and recognition from others. Campbell and Helen were well on their way to having both but the recognition they were receiving was only from colleagues within their own departments.

Stuart, and to a lesser extent Betty, were better respected at board level because they had proved themselves to be good at their core jobs. Alan was in limbo: people were not sure if he would hang on. Matthew seemed to be manipulating behind the scenes and Stuart knew that the rest of the team resented this. As far as Stuart could see, none of Matthew's fellow directors had any esteem for the young accountant.

Betty and Stuart had both worked for organizations where prizes and badges were given out at regular intervals to encourage recognition and formalise respect; but these hardly seemed right for the Vulcan board.

Personal fulfilment

This is the pinnacle of Maslow's Hierarchy of Needs. Here we develop our gifts and potential to the full and achieve personal growth through meeting challenges.

This need is often the most neglected in management and Stuart was the only manager at Vulcan even remotely close to fulfilling it.

Alan was poised just below this pinnacle, but there was no way he could actually reach the summit until Stuart acknowledged the situation.

Maslow used the term 'hierarchy' because he saw each need having to be fulfilled before it became important. In practice, there is no completely clear dividing line between these needs, and people usually make steady progress up the scale. However, movement up the ladder is not the only route. People can move downwards, too.

Where does Matthew fit?

Stuart pondered Maslow's concept and wondered about the rumours that Matthew had tried to make a pass at Betty. What need did this reveal?

The reality of Matthew's position, Stuart thought, was that Matthew felt anything but safe or secure at present; that he had dropped down the ladder and was now struggling to survive. He felt that his natural place was higher up and was making desperate bids to get there; making a pass at Betty might be a short-cut to esteem.

When Stuart looked ahead, he saw that the problem was likely to worsen. While Betty was rallying informal support for her position against Matthew's, Matthew was not.

Perhaps the team could not progress with him as a member.

*E*XERCISE

Look at the list below, assessing which items would be priorities among your subordinates. Score one point for the most important, two for the next, and so on.

Interesting work

Job security

Being appreciated for their work

Personal loyalty of supervisor

More money

Tactful discipline

Feeling involved

Promotion

Good working conditions

Help with personal problems

If you ranked more money and promotion as the two most important items, you are likely to be wrong, unless you are paying your staff a pittance. Offering your staff more money is not always a strong motivator. Results from recent research have shown that people are more likely to respond as follows:

Being appreciated for their work   (1)

Feeling involved   (2)

Help with personal problems   (3)

Job security   (4)

More money   (5)

Interesting work	⑥
Promotion	⑦
Personal loyalty of supervisor	⑧
Good working conditions	⑨
Tactful discipline	⑩

These results show managers could offer staff a wide variety of non-financial incentives, including:

● **Monthly awards:** Not just for the most successful salesperson, but also for the most improved salesperson, secretary, and so on.

● **Better working conditions:** improvements in office lay-out, desks, filing cabinets, carpets and other equipment.

● **Greater variety:** for example, in choice of company car.

● **More flexibility in working hours:** extra days off, longer lunches, permission to come in late or leave early.

● **Desirable jobs:** More (or less) travel, working with good people, special projects, training seminars or conferences.

● **More public recognition:** special awards, publications, reports in the monthly magazine.

● **Gifts:** birthday presents, and so on.

DANGERS OF CLONING IN SELECTION OF NEW STAFF

The Selection Officer believed that blue was the colour of truth.
The blue-eyed trainees therefore went to the responsible and sometimes
glamorous jobs, while the rest were tipped into the dustbin

From *Naples '44* by Norman Lewis

Helen had been busy since the meeting on her re-draft of the personnel policy (*case study 15*). Both she and Alan had been embarrassed by the conflict between Betty and Matthew. They also felt confused and hurt by Stuart's outburst. Alan simply wanted to keep a low profile, but Helen wanted to become more involved. She felt that the problems were in her area of specialization.

Helen had been growing steadily in stature over the past few months. She felt stimulated by Stuart and his recognition of what management theory could offer. This made her feel that she could act with increasing authority.

She set about recording the purpose of every remark made at board meetings, drawing a table that looked like this:

	WHY?	WHAT?	HOW?	IF?
Stuart	0	5	10	0
Matthew	15	2	1	8
Betty	10	4	1	15
Campbell	0	7	8	0

Alan had made no real contribution at this meeting, and she did not feel able to assess her own contribution objectively.

Her analysis was based on a system devised by David Kolb. He believes that there is a fundamental sequence of events that begins when people get together in order to achieve anything.

● They set out the problem – WHY? questions.

● They then look at the alternatives – WHAT? questions.

● They consider the practicalities – HOW? questions.

● Finally they consider the consequences of their proposals – IF? questions.

In Stuart's meeting, Betty and Matthew had stuck to asking WHY? questions, with Betty indulging, from time to time, in fantasies. Campbell and Stuart had demanded practical answers all the time. The result was chaos.

Helen wanted to get the board meetings working better; she asked each of her fellow directors to answer the following questionnaire. You should tackle it, too.

Questionnaire

Divide ten points between the responses to each situation.

Give the most points to the answer that best fits your way of thinking. Thus you might give seven points to the first response and one point to each subsequent response.

A You are asked to organize a project. List the following in *your* order of priority:

1 Look at why the project has been proposed.

2 Work out the exact requirements of the project.

3 Consider how the job is going to be completed.

4 Make sure you start on it as soon as possible.

B You are asked to write a detailed report for your boss on a pet project. Would you:

1 Try to stimulate his/her interest in the topic?

2 Ensure you extend his/her knowledge of the subject?

3 Present all the alternatives, rationally and cogently?

4 Clearly recommend courses for action?

C When you learn, are you:

1 Open to new experiences? ☐

2 Relying on your own observations? ☐

3 Trying to evaluate and reason things out? ☐

4 Looking to see the results of your work? ☐

D If you are faced with an unexpected crisis, do you:

1 Trust your feelings and try to get involved? ☐

2 Take your time before acting? ☐

3 Analyse the problem and try to work out how you can improve matters? ☐

4 Roll up your sleeves and dive headlong into the problem? ☐

Your total scores in response to question number one in each group are those a WHY? person would use; to number two, those a WHAT? person would use; number three a HOW? person and number four an IF? person.

This is how Vulcan's directors scored:

	WHY?	WHAT?	HOW?	IF?
Stuart	3	10	22	5
Matthew	25	10	0	5
Betty	15	3	0	22
Campbell	0	7	33	0
Helen	6	11	17	6
Alan	10	5	20	5

The figures show a remarkably similar pattern to those which Helen had compiled after the controversial meeting. Given control, Stuart had a fine potential team: Betty and Matthew on the crow's nest looking for ideas; Campbell plus Stuart being practical; Betty the enthusiast driving ideas to action.

Stuart was not surprised by Helen's results: they simply confirmed his concerns about Matthew and Betty, and his views on the need for balance in the team. Their discussion was broken up when Betty bounced in.

She explained that a Graham Bell she had met at a trade fair would be an ideal replacement for Doug Evans.

"He's just the man I've been looking for. Enthusiastic, good contacts, full of drive, great fun to be with..."

Helen's heart sank. She did not relish having to explain what she was discussing with Stuart. Both of them knew that Betty's attention span was less than five minutes.

"Doesn't that make him a bit too much like you?" asked Helen. "After all, Stuart has been hammering home the need for balance in a team. It seems to me you'll hire a carbon copy of yourself. It's not a salesman you want, but a reliable number two."

"Rubbish. My area is different from the rest of the business. It's not balance I'm after, it's more sales – that's what really balances the books."

Betty took a phone call from Stuart's desk and vanished at speed down the corridor.

Helen said: "The problem is, we only warm to people who speak our language. Betty likes talking to other WHY? and IF? people – they excite her."

"She frightens me," said Stuart.

"Exactly. You and Campbell are on the same wave-length. Betty is an exact opposite."

"I don't see Graham Bell complementing Betty. He sounds like a Betty clone."

"Unfortunately, unless we recruit professionally, we do recruit the people we get on with – clones."

"Always?"

"No, sometimes we realize that that we need someone to shake us up and take the first person that challenges us – regardless of anything else."

"Just as bad?"

"Worse."

Helen has a number of alternatives.

Option one

> Avoid interfering and let Betty recruit Graham Bell. After all, it is not as if they were recruiting a new director.

Verdict

Knowing what Helen knows about Betty and her department, this must be a worrying option. If the appointment works out as badly as Helen believes it will, Bell will be out within a year, having contributed very little. The cost for the company will have been high.

Option two

> Be present at the interview and try to steer Betty in the right direction.

Verdict

Certainly better than a snap appointment after a trade fair conversation. All the formalities would be observed and references would be taken up properly. Helen would know that having done their homework, Vulcan's chance of a good selection improves by more than 15 per cent.

Option three

> Insist Betty does a full job analysis, by making candiates complete questionnaires.

Helen believed that this would increase the chance of recruiting a sound external candidate by 40 per cent. She persuaded Stuart that the cost of such an exercise was worth it purely on cash grounds. Vulcan recruited 20 people a year, about half of whom stayed for more than three years and were regarded as successes. Looked at in this way, the cost of failure was stunning. By decreasing the chance of failure, Helen calculated that four out of the ten failures could be prevented. Stuart refused to take the figures as more than a guide, but accepted Helen's case.

Three weeks later, she told Stuart that Betty had decided not to appoint Graham Bell and had instead promoted Joe Wells, a taciturn Scot with an eye for detail.

Stuart was impressed and he and Helen agreed that interview training would be given to all managers concerned with selection.

*E*XERCISE

Look at your Kolb profile. Does it reflect how you communicate with others?

If so, what are the plus and minus points in your style?

How can you make improvements.

Think about your colleagues. How do they like to communicate?

Is there any way in which you could improve your existing lines of communication.

LISTENING TO THE TEAM

> Vision is the art of seeing things invisible
> Dr. Samuel Johnson

"Have you ever heard of TQM?" asked Helen.

Stuart was beginning to suspect that Helen knew more about management theory than he did.

"I'm glad you asked me about that." He was trying desperately to remember what the initials meant. Finally he said: "I've been meaning to have a word with you about TQM – of course everyone has got a different definition for it and yours might be different from mine. It's something to do with getting things right first time, isn't it?"

It was an educated guess; but Stuart was good at educated guesses. Helen told him in some detail about the concept. After a while, Stuart decided it was about time he took control of the conversation.

"Look Helen, I think it's essential that we listen to people within our team. That's why I've enjoyed our little chat today.

"Total Quality Management is a fascinating business concept and I'm all in favour of promoting it at Vulcan. We need to develop a new culture throughout the organization. But we don't want to confine these improvements to the management team alone.

"I don't think it's healthy if all the ideas percolate down from the top. There must be a large reservoir of good ideas among the rest of our staff. We need to tap into this resource and find their reactions to concepts like TQM for example.

"I want you to set aside some time for getting feedback from all levels of administration at Vulcan. That's about 20 people and would include all your personnel staff. See what their concerns are and how we can go forward from there."

Helen left Stuart with mixed feelings. She was pleased to be given the assignment: it was a challenge and Stuart's principles were close to her heart. But she had a nagging feeling that Stuart had manipulated her.

Her thoughts kept going back to a recent board meeting when Stuart had made the mysterious aside about the managers being better off in the near future.

Something was going on. Business at Vulcan was certainly improving; she knew that, but she did not like mysteries and she suspected that this project was part of it.

How does Helen go about listening to the administrative and personnel team at Vulcan?

There were a number of options open to her. For instance:

● She could create a suggestion box, or its equivalent. This would give staff the chance to air their grievances anonymously.

● Organize a competition: the winner to come up with the best idea for improving the company's image et cetera.

● Informal group discussions. Arrange to meet small groups for half-hour sessions to enable them to give their views on the company.

● One-to-one meetings in which she could listen in-depth to each individual's views.

Verdict

None of these options is suitable. Helen needed to create a procedure which would provide a channel of information which could be processed properly. It also needed to be re-usable.

Procedure

Helen got all the staff together and explained the issue.

"As you know, Vulcan has been undergoing considerable changes over the last six months. We've had some notable setbacks, but in general we are on course. We are thinking of making some fundamental changes to the way in which this organization runs. Not the least of these changes is greater involvement from all of you from now on.

"First, we want to know about the problems

you are currently facing and what we can do to make things better for all of us. We don't want you to pull your punches; there will be no recriminations. There are no Duncan Johnsons in the board room now.

"I have booked the training room for next Friday afternoon and I want everyone to attend.

"Before that, I have a short exercise for you all to complete. Just write down answers to the question 'What blocks and barriers do I have that prevent me being more effective as a member of the Vulcan team?'

"I would like everyone to think about this; don't discuss it with each other; come up with your personal list of answers. *I do not want to see your lists. I will not be present when your lists are discussed on Friday.*"

It is as well to run a dress rehearsal with, say, three selected supervisors if you want to carry out this process successfully.

Explain to them that their own group of five or six staff should sit round a table. Using a flip chart, each member of the group should read out in turn the first block or barrier from their personal list. When this personal block or barrier has been stated, each person at the table then says what they think about the issue.

Say the first statement is 'Lateness of the mail'. After this has been modified by the others round the table, the issue will become 'Trash mail confused with things that are important' and 'No afternoon mail'.

After the supervisor has provided the first issue and had it clarified, the process is repeated until all the statements have been dealt with.

In Vulcan's case, the groups might well come up with 50 issues between them, but some of these will overlap and some will be rejected outright.

The supervisors then ask their their groups to vote for the three issues they find most important.

The other groups are then shown these top three issues and invited to discuss whether they agree. The statements which attract the greatest consensus are then listed and classified under these headings:

PEOPLE

PROCESSES

PRODUCT

PLACE

PLANT

Finally, the manager in charge should justify the process by explaining that about 20 per cent of all problems are responsible for 80 per cent of all troubles. Work on the 20 and your administration will never be the same again.

CHECKLIST

When you want to hear from a team:

1 Check that there are no internal squabbles which could foul things up.
2 Take – and be seen to take – the issue seriously by sorting out the rooms, time and delegation.
3 Appoint helpers.
4 Be clear with your instructions – confusion can be disastrous.
5 Don't watch over the process.
6 Act on what is recommended.

*E*XERCISE

Sometimes managers need to speak directly to individual employees. They need to be good listeners if they want to build rapport and trust. If you want to sharpen up your listening skills, ask yourself these questions after you have held a discussion with your employees:

1 Did I understand each point they were trying to make?

2 Did I jump to any conclusions while they were still speaking?

3 Did I try to hunt for evidence that would prove them right/wrong while they were still talking?

4 Did I hunt for evidence that would prove my own point of view?

5 Did I let them speak for at least 50 per cent of the time?

6 Did I restate their ideas and feelings accurately?

7 Did I try to read their body language?

8 Did I read between the lines?

9 Did I show them that I was interested in listening to them?

THE
CREATIVE
MANAGER

APPRAISAL SYSTEMS

> All my shows are great. Some of them are bad. But they're all great.
> Lord Grade

One afternoon, Campbell called in Joe Riley and told him about his plans to introduce an appraisal system into production.

"Helen says it should help improve current performances and assess future career development..."

Campbell and Joe had known each other for a long time and his supervisor saw that this was the opportunity to tell Campbell the facts of life, at least as the shop floor saw them.

"Talking of appraisal systems, Campbell, people here have been appraising you and Helen. I don't know or care what's going on between you two, but it's difficult not to notice you've always got your heads together."

"For Chrissake…"

"Don't blow up, I'm simply saying what's on the grape vine. And I'm also saying that you'll have difficulty getting an appraisal scheme accepted if it's known to be coming from Helen."

Campbell rang Helen at home that evening and warned her about the rumours. She laughed and told him not to worry. She would have a word with her husband about it and suggested that Campbell do the same with his wife.

Campbell was not sure about that. His wife was something of a gossip and he guessed that if he told her about the rumours, it would only arouse her suspicion.

But Campbell was sure of one thing: he was more determined than ever to introduce an appraisal system into his department.

What should Campbell do?

Option one

> Tell key people that there was nothing in the rumour and forget about the appraisal scheme until the rumours died.

Verdict

Denying something only draws attention to the issue: 'no smoke without fire'. Helen and Campbell were not having an affair and it was inappropriate for them to let gossip get in the way of something as important as a new appraisal scheme.

Option two

> Stop seeing Helen.

Verdict

If he had, it might have caused increased suspicion. But both he and Helen should have acknowledged that people were talking. One way to do this would have been to bring others into the discussion: Joe Riley, for example, and someone else from personnel.

T HEORY

Introducing an appraisal scheme for judging staff performance can be fraught with problems unless the manager's standing is beyond question.

Campbell and Helen must win the confidence of their staff before having an appraisal; must assure them that the appraisal will benefit the organization and the individual alike.

Campbell needed to tell his staff exactly what an appraisal was:

> A procedure which collects, checks, shares and gives information about employees which can be used to improve their performance.

It is a tool to assist effective management. It does not assist, indeed it can amplify, poor management. It can make what has previously been accepted intolerable by bringing it out into the open.

An effective appraisal scheme must be clear in its purpose.

Purposes can include:

- Assessing training and development needs.

- Helping to improve current performance.

- Motivating staff to reach organization standards and objectives.

- Reviewing past performance.

- Assessing future potential.

- Succession planning.

- Assessing increases in salary.

- Checking the effectiveness of selection techniques.

Appraisal cannot possibly do all these things at once – many of them are incompatible. Salary, for instance, can be so important to people that it overrides everything else.

Who benefits from appraisals? Campbell saw his system as a formal review of the past year's work and a chance to set standards and targets for the coming year. He wanted an appraisal once a year, six months from the salary review.

Top-down involvement:
Campbell told Stuart about the plan, and together with Helen the three of them reviewed the motive for having an appraisal. Campbell was anxious that it should not be seen as an infringement of privacy or a form of organizational spying. That would make the workforce resent the scheme. The information provided was to become part of a Vulcan data bank.

Stuart agreed, but insisted that Helen have access to the results. "If other departments decide to have the appraisals, I need to make sure that what you do is not different from, say, what marketing and accounting do."

Resources, time, training:
The scheme now had backing from the top and Campbell was given a budget. Joe Riley was put in charge of the detail. He and Helen came up with a proposal for an appraisal training course, to show managers and supervisors with no previous experience how to run appraisal

schemes succesfully. It would be exactly tailored to the needs of production and run in-house by a consultant recommended by Helen.

Emphasis on the people aspects – minimising bureaucracy:
The focus of Campbell's appraisal was to be on individual development, which meant relatively little paperwork. This benefited all concerned – the interviewer and the interviewee.

Prepare carefully, monitor continuously and be prepared to modify.
Joe and Helen prepared well and the appraisals were an immediate success with the supervisors and foremen. However, they were a big disappointment on the shop floor. Joe realized that there were a number of reasons for this, including: high staff turnover – about 17 per cent; shift working, and, most important, the numbers involved. For the moment, the shop floor appraisal scheme was dropped.

CHECKLIST

The most important points to remember are:

1 Nothing new should come out of an appraisal interview. Instead, confirm what has already been understood. Anything which comes as a shock could spell trouble. "That's the first time you've told me about that..." is likely to start the sparks flying.

2 Appraisal is just one more element in effective management – it is not a system imposed to rectify faults.

3 The system should have a built-in capacity for change and development. You simply cannot predict how the appraisal system will be working in five years time.

Some tips for managers running their first appraisal:

Take the job seriously – even if it is 'just another job' to you, it is likely to be important for the person facing you.

● Have all relevant paperwork to hand.

● Ensure privacy and avoid interruptions.

● Emphasise the importance of the individual – cut down formality.

Be prepared for criticism of appraisal interviews and interviewers.

- Let the interviewee have his/her say.

- Don't guide, listen – be a pair of ears and not a mouth (*case study 10*).

- Don't defend the organization when the employee raises a critical point.

Always try to give constructive feedback.

- Refer only to behaviour that can be changed.

- Be specific and descriptive.

- Offer alternatives.

- Leave the employee with a choice of action.

Think SMART: appraisals should be:

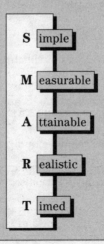

S imple

M easurable

A ttainable

R ealistic

T imed

*E*XERCISE

Here is how you can prepare for a performance appraisal.

1 What is my core job (*case study 14*) – do I meet these requirements?

2 What do I like best about my job?

3 What do I like least?

4 What have I achieved in the last 12 months?

5 In which areas have I failed?

6 Who could help me improve my performance – apart from myself?

7 What blocks and barriers exist within the organization which hinder my effectiveness?

8 How could I improve my performance?

9 What do I expect to be doing in three and five years time?

10 Are these goals attainable?

11 Do I need more experience or training to further my development?

12 What new goals and standards do I require from now on?

A PLAN FOR PERSONAL DEVELOPMENT

If you wish to drown, do not torture yourself with shallow water

Bulgarian proverb

Helen was grateful for Campbell's warning about the rumours of their supposed affair (*case study 24*). She realized that she had been spending too much time with Campbell and was relieved when Alan approached her for help. It took the spotlight off her and Campbell and she was genuinely interested in helping Alan, who had a new problem. He had been taking a visitor on a guided tour of the accounts department when he found the computer room unmanned except for three juniors, who were sitting idle around the coffee machine. Alan had to get the visitor away as fast as he could.

He returned two hours later, and still the computer room was idle. Furious, he demanded:

"Right, Bill, what's going on?"

"Mary was taken sick yesterday and some idiot's logged off wrongly. Wiped the main hard disk."

"What's it got to do with Mary? Don't you all know how to log off? Has anyone rung the maintenance contractor?"

"Mary's the only one who understands the network."

Recognizing that this was essentially a personnel problem which could only be remedied by training more people to run the system, Alan consulted Helen.

What advice could she give?

Option one

> Deal with the immediate emergency and suggest that Mary train an assistant.

Verdict

Having just one, or even two, 'experts' entrusted with vital understanding of a key part of the organization can be dangerous. Even if Mary trained an assistant, this new person might cause more problems than they solved. Juniors entrusted with key responsibility arouse jealousy and mistrust. They may also start demanding higher status than their position merits.

People lose motivation if their jobs depend on a piece of equipment which they don't understand and cannot control. They become, in effect, less important than the equipment.

Staff cannot be expected to know and perform more than routine maintenance procedures; but the more staff are aware of these, the better. Calling in the experts at the slightest breakdown is wasteful. Most faults are easily fixed and many are avoidable.

Option two

> Set up a training programme and have everyone attend.

Verdict

A good idea, as far as it goes. This is what Helen advised in order to meet the immediate problem. The programme was run by Mary on the first Saturday morning of each month, using training material supplied by the contractors.

The objective of the course was 'to give all those with direct access to the computer network an understanding of the strengths and limitations of the system, of basic operating procedures with emphasis on signing on and off, and the remedial actions possible for common errors and faults'. All the accounts staff completed the course and most of them benefited.

Option three

> After the immediate problem has been sorted out, perhaps Alan should introduce a systematic development programme for all his staff.

Verdict

This has to happen as soon as possible if Vulcan is to grow and its managers are not to waste time fire-fighting.

THEORY

Every job requires three attributes:

Aptitude A one-legged actor, however blond or muscular, has no aptitude for the role of Tarzan. Obvious? Yes, but very poorly qualified people are recruited the whole time. We know of trainee draughtsmen who cannot visualise in three dimensions, and of telephone salespersons with stutters.

Helen knew that numeracy was an essential aptitude of the accounts floor, as was doggedness. She used simple tests to eliminate candidates who hadn't the right aptitude.

Skills required for accounts staff included accurate adding and subtracting; following a system; using a keyboard. People's skills – given that they have the right potential – can be developed by training. Skills are measurable and can be monitored. Unless managers offer staff the chance to develop their skills, they will stagnate.

Knowledge required to complete the job. This can range from knowing where things are kept to whom to ask for help. Staff need to be given the chance to be self-starters. Treat people as if they have brains, and they can grow in their jobs. If Alan's operators know the background of the data they are preparing, they can suggest improvements to the system.

Analysis
Helen considered junior and middle management, and Alan and Betty themselves.

She interviewed them about their management jobs and came up with a set of skills necessary for survival at the appropriate level, it being assumed that each level possessed the skills of the preceding levels.

In the case of Alan's department, the aptitudes, skills and knowledge were:

Aptitudes

- Numeracy
- Doggedness
- Precision

Skills

- Adding, subtracting
- Using the system
- Facility with a keyboard

Knowledge

- How to log off the spread sheet program
- How the program was designed
- How the program would cope if Vulcan's turn-over increased dramatically

Helen discussed this list with Stuart and checked it against those prescribed for businesses of similar size in the same field. With the list authenticated in this way, it could claim to be a respectable standard by which to measure people at Vulcan.

Next, Helen suggested to Stuart that Vulcan introduced a development programme. It would, in fact, be based on the appraisal scheme described in *case study 24*, and on the list of skills, aptitude and knowledge described above. Helen drafted a form for use by interviewers. It clearly defined the ideal level for the skill in question and provided a scoring sytem, easy to apply, for the level of skill reached by each individual.

Stuart complemented Helen on her work and asked her to keep the idea on ice until next year. He felt that Vulcan was not quite ready for such a scheme: until the business was ready to expand again, training might cause discontent – the potential for career advancement was simply not there.

EXERCISE

Have a look at the management skills that Helen developed for Vulcan and consider how well they fit your own organization. What additional skills are needed?

■ Look at your own recruitment policy. What mechanisms do you use to select people with the correct balance of skills?

■ Is there such a thing as career progression in your organization? If it is not based on additional skills, how could such a scheme be introduced?

■ How would you rate your own skills at your present level in the organization? What could you do to develop a higher set of skills to ensure that you are ready for promotion?

DOING THE RIGHT THING AT THE RIGHT TIME

> Those who are unhappy have no need for anything in this world but people capable of giving them their attention.
>
> Simone Weil, *L'Attente de Dieu*, 1949

Campbell arrived at work sensing an uneasy atmosphere. Before he could sit down, there was a knock at his door, and Mike Coombes, a supervisor, shuffled in looking embarrassed.

"Well?"

"We've got a problem. I tried to contact you yesterday but it was too late, you'd already left."

Campbell had known the supervisor for a long time. Mike was a man who often got agitated and preferred to delegate upward at the first sign of trouble. The snag was you never knew when the trouble was really serious.

"Roger fell down drunk at work yesterday."

"Just like that?"

"Well, we all know that he likes a drink, especially since his wife left him. But he's never been like this before. He has to look after the children you know and one of them is in hospital..." As Mike went on, Campbell realized that there was a real problem.

Mike was waiting for a response.

What should Campbell do?
He has three main options:

Option one

> Tell Mike Coombes to carry on and report to Campbell on any new developments.

Verdict This is not delegation, but abdication.

Option two

> Drop everything and become fully involved.

Verdict Many managers find it tempting to give immediate attention to exciting events at the expense of more routine and mundane jobs. This particular problem is quite complex and could get worse if not handled correctly.

Option three

> Buy time in order to think out a plan of action.

Verdict The best option.

THEORY

Managers put themselves under great strain trying to solve the wrong problems. The secret of avoiding such stress is knowing what your job is – your purpose; understanding which problems are your responsibility; and structuring your time effectively – determining priority.

Once purpose, responsibility and priority have been settled, a manager can usefully look at the objectives he or she has in solving the particular problem and the tactics that might be employed to achieve these objectives.

Purpose
Vulcan's purpose is to reduce its bank loan, return to trading at the best possible profit level, then to expand. Campbell's own purpose exists in relation to Vulcan's: to hold the technical activities of the company together so that it can carry on producing efficiently.

Responsibility
It follows, as far as Campbell is concerned, that anything threatening (or helping) Vulcan's ability to produce is at the heart of Campbell's responsibility. The drunken Roger could threaten production, and so he is a prime responsibility. It would be wrong to step back and leave Roger's friends to arrange for him to visit a counsellor or Alcoholics Anonymous. That much is obvious, provided the basic thinking about purpose and responsibility has been clearly worked out.

But should Campbell act in isolation, or should he consult Stuart? Or perhaps he should delegate the problem to Mike Coombes, giving him very clear instructions on how the matter should be handled? If Campbell has correctly defined his responsibility, what he does in this case has already been delegated to him by Stuart. So he should not bother Stuart.

Mike Coombes is certainly responsible for the running of Process Room Three, where Roger fell down. The drunk endangered the running of Room Three, so perhaps Coombes should take over the problem? If Room Three was not an essential part of Vulcan's process – if it was, say, a store room for cleaning materials – then Campbell might well delegate the entire problem.

But of course, the problem is Campbell's, because if Room Three stops work, which it did after Roger collapsed, Vulcan's production experiences a hiccup. Accepting that the drunk is Campbell's problem puts it on Campbell's list with plenty of other things to achieve that day. He cannot do them all, so he has to establish priorities.

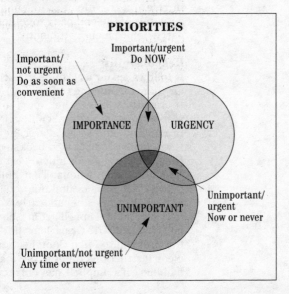

PRIORITIES

Important/urgent
Do NOW

Important/
not urgent
Do as soon as
convenient

IMPORTANCE   URGENCY

Unimportant/
urgent
Now or never

UNIMPORTANT

Unimportant/not urgent
Any time or never

Importance is the problem's power to prevent the organization achieving its purpose.

Urgency is about time. Problems which are both urgent and important demand priority.

Important jobs with low urgency can be planned for a later date; urgent jobs with low importance need to be done straight away or not at all. The lowest of the four categories – non-urgent and non-important – can be done or not done as the mood takes.

Roger's drunkenness had certainly been both important and urgent for Mike Coombes yesterday. Today, because Mike Coombes responded quickly, the urgency has disappeared, but the problem remains important. Just how important depends on what else Campbell must achieve today. He has a board meeting in ten minutes. To be late would waste the time of several other busy people, besides which, the meeting is where he must make his contribution to ensuring the company's survival. Campbell therefore says to Coombes:

"OK Mike, I have a board meeting until twelve. If he is drunk again this morning, get me out of the meeting. Otherwise I'll expect you in my office at twelve, when we'll sort it out."

EXERCISE

1 Write down your organization's objective in one or two short sentences, but no more.

2 Write down your own responsibility in fulfilling that objective, in one sentence.

3 Think of a problem, such as one of your staff regularly arriving back from lunch too drunk to complete the day's work.

4 Is it your responsibility? Should you handle it in isolation, or involve others, up or down the ladder of responsibility?

5 If it is your responsibility, rate its importance and urgency.

6 When will you sort it out?

Having put this much clear thought into the matter, capitalize on the effort by making it an opportunity to define objectives and tactics.

Remember that objectives need to be screened against responsibilities.

Campbell might list the following:

● Helping Roger to get over his problem.

● Re-emphasizing the company rules on alcohol.

● Giving Roger a formal warning.

● Sacking Roger.

● Starting an anti-drink campaign in Vulcan.

But the most pressing objective of all is to ensure that the problem never happens again. To meet this, the choice is between warning Roger not to arrive drunk, or to fire him. Roger's skill as a programmer will take time to replace, so Campbell decided that it was in Vulcan's interests to give Roger a second, but final, chance.

So his primary objective is to discipline Roger for the offence and warn him that for any re-occurrence, he will be fired. His second objective will certainly include helping Roger – if help is required and welcomed. Reminding staff of the company rules on drink can wait.

Finally, Campbell decided on tactics. Campbell's choice was a short disciplinary interview. If Roger accepted that warning, Campbell would ask him to go and see Helen in Personnel. Helen, with whom Campbell had discussed the event, was in no doubt that any counselling that might be needed was her responsibility.

STRUCTURED PROBLEM SOLVING

> We are all continually faced with a series of great opportunities brilliantly disguised as insoluble problems
>
> John W. Gardner

Betty had to admit, grudgingly, that she had been impressed by the way Helen and her team had analysed the blocks and barriers which were reducing their efficiency. Betty now wanted try it out for herself. It might be a way of getting some fresh marketing ideas.

She called in all her staff and announced that they were to drop everything and do some brainstorming.

"I want all your fresh marketing ideas, however mad. I'll write them on this flip chart. OK, first idea..."

It was like drawing teeth and most of the group simply froze. They had never attended a brainstorming session before and most of them did not understand what they were supposed to be doing.

The first few ideas were very mundane:
- Sell to schools.
- Use faster chips.
- Have more agents.

Betty, who had promised them she would not interfere, and was there only to write down the proposals, kept butting in, scoffing at ideas she thought worthless and favouring ones she had always advocated. One by one, her team fell silent. Betty was left to stop the session with nothing achieved, and feeling foolish. When she had recovered, she went to see Helen.

"It worked for you, so why didn't it work for me? They are supposed to be creative and all we got was the same old things."

What should Helen suggest?

Option one | Run another brainstorming session herself.

Verdict Not a bad idea: she could not do worse than Betty. But this would upset Betty just when she was trying, for a change, to organize her team rather than allow it to muddle through.

Option two

> Send Betty on a course.

Verdict

Plenty of good courses would be available and Betty would have enjoyed learning how to do things properly; but this would slow down Betty's impetus; she might lose interest completely.

Option three

> Work alongside Betty in a brainstorming session.

Verdict

This meets the need for training Betty and getting immediate results. But there are two problems:

● Betty is probably the wrong person in any case to run the session. People just don't feel spontaneous enough with their bosses for this kind of activity to work.

● Simply collecting ideas for the sake of collecting ideas is a useless activity. Betty, Matthew and Alan found this out in case study 20, when they presented their ragbag of ideas to Stuart.

Option four

> Set up a formal, planned and costed exercise to look at all aspects of innovation in Vulcan: an innovation search. This would include a brainstorming session, but only as part of the exercise. The search is about the total process of innovation, not just the exciting conception stage.

Verdict

A bold and imaginative step. Vulcan depends on new ideas for its survival and such an important function should hardly be confined to an unplanned Monday morning.

THEORY

Vulcan may be a hi-tech company, but its need to cultivate ideas is beset with the same sort of problems that affect the oldest industry in the world – farming. Which crops will flourish in which fields is common knowledge and farmers rarely waste their time planting seeds which have produced a poor yield in the past. Finding a truly viable new crop requires a far-reaching search, not just for the new crop, but for economical ways of growing it.

Running an innovation search

A full innovation search takes in everything required to nurture new ideas; it involves everyone; and one of its best features is the protection of delicate new ideas at the conception stage so that sceptics may not dismiss them before they have a chance to develop into practical proposals.

● The initial stage, taking about a month, is devoted to refining an initial crude statement of the search's goal.

● The next stage, taking about three months, is the search itself, requiring specialized work, and must be formally budgetted.

An exact costing was impossible at this stage, but Helen got some data from Campbell about a previous, broadly similar exercise, in order to give Stuart an idea of what the commitment was likely to be.

Then, it was essential to decide how the innovation search should be co-ordinated. Betty was obviously the manager with the appropriate authority. But was she the right person to coordinate the project? The co-ordinator needed to be a tactful person who knew Vulcan well and was not seen as a threat by other managers.

Option one

> Betty, Helen or one of the other directors should be appointed the co-ordinator.

Verdict

In practice, senior managers are too busy to give this job the concentration it requires. Also, senior managers can inhibit juniors, who may tell them what they believe they want to hear, rather than what they really think.

Option two

> Bring in an outside consultant.

Verdict

This is a safe choice, but it costs money. The consultant will need to learn about the business.

Option three

> Select a creative junior manager with the appropriate personality, brief him or her thoroughly, and provide back-up from above when necessary.

Verdict

This is what Helen recommended. Betty delegated the job to Melanie, one of her marketing assistants. She had charm, was full of ideas and, above all, she threatened no one.

Helen gave Melanie precise instructions and added, "Betty and I have cleared it with Stuart Blyth that you can have the attention of anyone you choose. But remember, everyone is busy; they'll help, provided you don't get pushy."

In order to launch the innovation search, Melanie then worked through the following steps:

What is the goal?
Stuart defined it as: 'To find new products which will bring back to life Vulcan's ageing

portfolio of products, in particular the mini-computer range whose sales life is nearly exhausted.'

What are the constraints?

Set about refining this initial, crudely-stated objective by discussing, with all the key managers, what would be the limitations on new ideas. Work systematically through six headings:

1 Who has the final right of veto over the ideas that emerge?

Betty had been delegated the search by Stuart, but Matthew was also involved. Would he keep knocking ideas on the head for reasons of cost? This was put to Stuart,who gave an unequivocal reply: "It's up to marketing to come up with ideas that will satisfy me. If the others want to help, that's fine, in fact I'd like that, but at the end of the day it's marketing's job, and marketing's veto."

Often, in less effective organizations than Vulcan, the co-ordinator of an innovation search has to report to a committee, which adopts politically acceptable ideas, not the best ideas.

2 Financial

Any new idea must be judged for its potential benefit, cost and risk. Matthew came up with a rule of thumb for initially assessing the benefit/risk ratio which Melanie found alarming: a new Vulcan product needs to be able to sell 8,000 in the first year in order to cover the development, finance and other costs. Melanie thought that this was a large number and that almost every new idea would die at birth. But after hearing from Alan and Matthew the cost of Vulcan's bank borrowing, she accepted it as a realistic target.

$\boxed{3}$ Time

How soon did the ideas need to be implemented? The mini-computer range was to be withdrawn in the spring and the bank was expecting its revenue to be partially replaced in the following year's balance sheet.

$\boxed{4}$ Staff

Stuart could not recruit new staff; he was, in fact, expecting to shed about 50 people – 10 per cent of Vulcan's workforce – during the next year. This meant that some Vulcan staff would need to be retrained in certain skills because the company could not afford to buy in expertise from outside.

Helen also realized that some of the graduates Campbell had recruited in the last three years could well be used more effectively in an enlarged new product section. It was an idea that she had not considered before which made her realize, not for the first time, that systematic questioning forces managers to think.

$\boxed{5}$ Company morale and general trading conditions

The economic climate was harsh, but everyone involved had the will to make Vulcan succeed. However, the proposed redundancies might change this position.

$\boxed{6}$ Legal

Various arms embargoes were likely to remain or become stricter. Stuart emphasized that Vulcan could not get involved in more defence work. So all new ideas had to be for the general consumer market.

Redefining the goal

It took Melanie many visits to the senior

managers to agree on a new defintion of the goal in the light of these restraints. Eventually, Melanie got Stuart and Betty to agree that in reality the goal should be:

> To provide Stuart Blyth with recommendations for new products for Vulcan. The volume of the new products shipped must be able to compensate for the 6 per cent loss in turnover due to the expected 20 per cent fall in factory gate prices across the industry and the decrease in revenue from old lines, especially the ageing mini-computer line. The new products must be ready for delivery in the next year and achieve full volume in 18 months. Unless a substantial financial case can be made, the new products must be developed using existing resources of people and money.

Stuart, understanding the detail of the financial issues, began further discussions with Alan, Matthew and the bank.

If an innovation search is not integrated with the realities facing an organization, it is at best wasteful and at worst destructive. The preparatory work necessary to prepare an intelligent and refined statement of objective is worth all the effort people can give it.

*E*XERCISE

> Take any brief you have been given and redefine it against the six restraints listed above.

LOOKING FOR OPPORTUNITIES

> An artificial novelty is never as effective as a repetition that manages to suggest a fresh truth
> Marcel Proust

Betty had come round to the idea of the innovation search, but she still felt frustrated by its slow progress. She wanted to get to the brainstorming session, but had to wait until Stuart had agreed to the refined statement of objectives. When it was eventually passed, she said: "I could have told you that on day one." Matthew observed: "Why didn't she, then?"

Betty was further frustrated at the next day's board meeting when Helen "pedantically" proposed alternative methods for generating, or collecting, ideas. Which do you think best?

Option one

> Invite ideas, written down in a clear form, asking for them to be delivered to Betty's office. In effect, a 'suggestions box'.

Verdict Suggestions schemes can be productive but

people tend to play safe, proposing improvements in what already exists. The 'suggestion box' not only inhibits creativity, but does not allow crude ideas to be built upon. Most good ideas start life as raw sparks of intuition. Their flaws are overcome by teamwork.

Option two

> The brainstorming exercise: sessions by individuals from all over Vulcan.

Verdict

Obviously a good way to proceed, *BUT* for Vulcan (and most organizations) it will work best if it opens with a presentation of ideas already available from within Vulcan's various departments. There are probably dozens of ideas around Vulcan that have never been presented in the right atmosphere. Starting a brainstorming with these is the best stimulus we know for getting fresh ideas to grow.

Melanie therefore asked Vulcan's technical team to give quick presentations of their existing ideas, with the emphasis on demonstrating Vulcan's edge in the technology. The whole of the board was present, plus all staff remotely connected with or interested in product development. At the end of the session, Melanie rose and said: "That's Vulcan's existing bank of ideas. Tomorrow, we are going to add to it." Before Betty could get to her feet to speak, Stuart and the other directors were on their way back to their offices.

The session
The same people were present. Melanie had prepared a brief, which she handed to everyone, with a list of simple rules:

1 Suspend judgement, no criticism.

2 Produce plenty of ideas; don't worry about quality at this stage.

3 Listen to other people's ideas and be prepared to build on them.

4 Freewheel with your ideas – use all your experience, not just your expertise at work.

She also wrote at the top of the flip chart:

New product ideas to ensure the future prosperity of Vulcan.

As the ideas came out, Melanie wrote them down on the flip chart, numbering as she went. As the sheets were filled, she stuck them up on the walls. Discussion was confined to clarifying language. Idea number 15 came from Stuart: 'Sell computers to camel riders, with software to monitor how long the water will last in different drought conditions.' Everyone collapsed into giggles. Melanie asked them to vote on the worst idea so far. Stuart's camels won.

She then said:

"However, there might be one good aspect to his idea. There usually is." Soon, the concept of using computers for monitoring was under discussion. When 50 ideas had been collected and posted, Melanie, with Helen and Betty's backing, asked whether they should continue the exercise and involve departments all round Vulcan. The session had lasted 50 minutes. Subsequently, Melanie organized sessions in every department, involving up to 12 people. In departments where there was no technical expertise, she ensured that the sessions began with a quick presentation of Vulcan's technical strengths, and then an expert was present for the rest of the session. After four sessions there were about 100 ideas, 30 of which were judged to have potential. These 30 were then sent round to the three main departments – production, marketing and finance – with the following questions in large type at the end of the list:

> Could you make it?

> Could you sell it?

> Could you make money out of it?

The departments were asked to judge the ideas according to their expertise on a scale of one to five, one being hopeless and five being perfect. Judgement was to be based on gut feeling, without going into details. Melanie incorporated the comments that came in, expanding the top 3 concepts from two or three words on the flip chart to around 100 words. In this form, they could be discussed without apology. A set of three ideas came out top. Provisional patents were taken out on two ideas and the third, basically a marketing concept for repackaging existing hardware and software, seemed to offer immediate possibilities.

Melanie's role was coming to an end and Betty was gradually taking over. The two patented ideas would be developed over a six-month period.

The third was an electronic notebook for students. It was to be small and run off rechargeable batteries and it could have several functions. It could be used to take notes and then, using a parallel display with the notes on one side of the screen and the 'fair' copy on the other, could be used to write up a neat, finished version. It would have a cheap printer attached, and would plug directly into college or university equipment. Secondly, it would also have a program to cross-reference key words and phrases for essay writing and literature study. Language and grammar program packs would be made available.

The idea had grown from two words, 'electronic notebook', uttered by Alan at the first session. Betty had immediately said: "Yes – for students – the market's wide open."

Campbell and Alan had then built up the rest of the specification, with some input from Melanie and other juniors in Betty's department. Stuart's eyes had lit up as the concept developed, but he had remained silent, just nodding his head – a low-key contribution which none the less had heightened everyone's confidence and enthusiasm.

Campbell saw no problems in producing the necessary volume. Sales of 40,000 would be needed in the second year to meet the necessary low price of the product. The revenue target would be met, provided costs could be controlled by importing part-finished materials at the right price. There was also a worry about getting the software at the right price. But what spurred them on was Betty's confidence, backed by comments from her principal wholesalers, that the sales volume was relatively easy to achieve. If anything, Betty worried that it might be too good and that Vulcan's larger competitors would move in before Vulcan had recovered its development costs.

Meanwhile, Matthew was working overtime. He had noticed a few errors of calculation in Betty's revenue projection and was busy with his own set of figures: the opportunity, he thought, to regain his due status. He would let Betty present her figures to the board, then pounce.

*E*XERCISE

Try to figure out who, in your organization, you would appoint as the co-ordinator of an innovation research. They must be:

● Able to work full-time on the project.

● Able to deal with all levels of the organization.

● Not seen as a threat or over-ambitious.

● Enthusiastic and intelligent.

● Willing to be trained in brainstorming and analysis.

● Able to communicate well in written and spoken presentations.

● Able to establish objectives for the project by working with top management.

● Able to analyse and collate the data.

TACKLING 'INTRACTABLE' PROBLEMS

> Give me somewhere to stand and I will move the earth
>
> Archimedes (287-212 B.C.)

Matthew, thanks to Helen's insistence that all senior management were involved in the key stages of the innovation search, couldn't complain that he had been ignored. But he still felt that his talents had not been properly utilized. He could not wait to see Betty's formal proposal for the launch of the electronic notebook. One lunchtime he sneaked into her office and took a furtive look at her first draft. He was disappointed with what he saw and thought: 'I'm sure I can improve on this.' He saw himself as the only person in Vulcan with a blend of both imagination and tactical business sense. He thought that he was a master of project costing; he was going to use his advantage. He went back to his office and wrote his own 20-page proposal. The result, he was convinced, was far superior to Betty's effort. It was a wide-ranging document, covering costings and marketing. His plan was to let Betty make her presentation to the board, then eclipse it with his own.

Betty's 'effort' was brilliantly presented and made an immediate impression on the others.

Helen was especially pleased that Betty's dynamism was tempered with convincing first-hand evidence, gained from Vulcan's main wholesale and retail customers, that the sales predictions were, if anything, conservative. When the initial excitement had died down, Matthew got up: "Betty: your figures on page 27 – costing for semi-finished parts from Taiwan – are you sure you're not being over-optimistic?" Both Betty and Alan, who had worked from the prices given them by Matthew, looked confused. Betty dropped her glasses. "You're calculating the component price at today's rate. But if you allow a proper contingency for currency fluctuation, then of course the revenue target takes significantly longer to reach." Stuart asked Betty to check her figures again. On his way out, Matthew presented each member of the board with his own launch plan, in a special folder bearing his initials. "I think you will find these figures more accurate," he said quietly. Betty said, not so quietly, "*YOU BASTARD*."

Next morning, Betty's resignation, also in a folder bearing her initials, was on Stuart's desk. It read simply: "I quit. Betty."

If you were Stuart, what would you do?

Option one

> Shrug your shoulders and accept Betty's resignation?

Verdict

Of course, Betty was too important to be allowed to leave over a relatively trivial matter. What is more, she did have a grievance. She had prepared her proposal on figures originally provided by Matthew. Now he had changed the goalposts.

Option two

> Refuse to accept Betty's resignation and hope that things eventually work out between her and Matthew?

Verdict It had gone too far for that. Two board members were at war and Betty was not likely to keep it private. There was a real danger that the team would break down into factions.

Option three Insist that Betty stay and sack Matthew instead? This was clearly the point of Betty's move.

Verdict It was also Stuart's gut reaction. But had Matthew really done anything wrong? If Stuart dismissed him for aggravating Betty, Matthew would argue, with some justice, that he had been acting in Vulcan's interests, and that a little damage to Betty's pride was an insignificant price to pay. And Matthew's criticism of Betty's figures, though presented in the wrong way, was valid. It would be necessary, in the current economic climate, to give the bank an ultra-conservative estimate of when the revenue target would be met. Not only this but Betty had over-reacted, and Matthew would be justified in pointing this out.

Option four Call in the directors not involved in the problem – Alan, Helen and Campbell – and share his concerns?

Verdict He didn't want to fall into Campbell's trap and form his own boardroom A-team (case study 16). He wanted to develop a real team at Vulcan.

Option five Bring in a management consultant as counsellor.

Verdict No guarantee of success, but probably the best in the circumstances. This was an A1 decision (*case study 18*): Stuart did not need information to make a better decision; he needed help to reach a decision at all.

THEORY

The counsellor, a professional recommended by Helen, had a single philosophy: to ask Stuart to define the elements of the problem, then treat each of them in turn.

Stage one: **splitting the problem into sub-problems.** The consultant asked Stuart to brainstorm (*case study 27*) different ways of stating the problem. He was asked to begin each statement with the words 'How do I'. Stuart's list had 20 items, including:

- How do I deal with Betty's resignation?
- How do I improve the communication between departments?
- How do I get over my mistrust of Matthew and my dislike of Betty's behaviour?
- How do I limit the damage of the public row?
- How do I get them to work together and compete but not stand on each others' toes?
- How do I get Betty not to smoke in my office?
- How do I deal with the Matthew problem in the long term?

It was quite obvious to Stuart when he had finished the list why he had become bogged down. With some twenty sub-problems, it had been impossible for him to concentrate on one. The counsellor noted the way Stuart mentioned the Matthew problem, but reserved it for later. Next, the consultant asked Stuart to identify which items on the list were trivia, and which were important.

Stage two: **classifying the sub-problems.** Betty had some annoying habits, including her jokes about not being able to smoke in his office, but these, in terms of the survival of the Vulcan team, are neither important not urgent. Stuart happily left them aside. By contrast, the resignation must be dealt with. The fact that the board was likely to be split was probably less immediate, but certainly none the less worrying. Inter-departmental communications were essential, but relatively long-term. And so on.

Stage three: **solutions.** The counsellor began by asking Stuart to forget all but the most urgent sub-problem. There was obviously no possibility in Stuart's mind of fudging the issue, and so the consultant asked for 'ways of getting through or over'. Stuart proposed asking Betty to hold her resignation for a week while he discussed guidelines of responsibility with Matthew, and the others.

By this time, Stuart had virtually taken over the session from the consultant. Like anyone with an independent turn of mind, who from an early age had been taught to think for themselves, he was fundamentally cynical of management consultants. He had only called in this specialist because he felt too close to the situation; and because he mistrusted his judgement – it seemed to be polluted with negative personal feelings about Betty and mistrust of Matthew.

Now, she seemed determined to re-assert herself ('earn her fee'), and returning to the list of 20 problems, she pedantically insisted that Stuart sort the problems into groups:

■ resignation
■ demarcations
■ board conflicts
■ new product strategy...
■ and finally Matthew.

She asked Stuart to say for each group what he intended to do and give a time scale for action. Stuart found the process painfully slow and simplistic. When he got down to the last category – Matthew – he felt so impatient for something decisive to come out of the exercise that he said: "He has to go, and the sooner the better." The consultant said: "I never promised to do your thinking for you; but I did say I would make it easier for you to make up your mind."

 XERCISE

Any major problem that has been with you for some time tends to make your mind seem to flit about.

Try to imagine a work poblem of your own which would require outside help. Given that no consultant can ever make up your mind for you, what kind of problem justifies the expense?

You have three choices in using the concepts of this case study: you may be able to think clearly enough to set the problem out into subsets yourself, you may need an outside counsellor to discipline your thoughts, or you may not have enough information in your own head to come to useful conclusions. In the latter case the technique may be used with a group of 'helpers' and you as the problem owner. The counsellor role now changes to become a chairperson maximizing the effectiveness of the 'helpers' in the analysis of the problem and the provision of solutions.

Work through the problem and do not forget to complete formal action plans – what you are going to do and exactly when you will do it.

CHANGE-

INTRODUCING SWEEPING CHANGE

Campbell was rereading Betty's proposals for the electronic
notebook. He was not an excitable man, but the implications
of what he read left him gasping. His understanding of the
technology told him that a speech interface was feasible;
and now his own graduate trainee, Roger Tasken, was
proposing a whole range of add-ons that could give the
product at least ten years' life. Talking with Tasken,
impeccably dressed in a three-piece pin-stripe suit with a
flower in the button hole, made Campbell feel old, and his
mind was in overdrive as he walked back to his office: it was
not just the commercial opportunity which was making his

mind race; it was the enormity of the change that the new development would impose.

His three shift supervisors – Joe Riley, Mike Coombes and Roger Partridge – were waiting for him when he came in. They came straight to the point:

"We understand that you are going to stop making things here."

"What?"

"If you think we are going to let Duncan Johnson's factory be a packing station for imports, you must be crazy."

Campbell played instinctively for time. He allowed them to talk on, making a compulsory grunt here and there, and agreed that 'he had heard what they had had to say and that he would give it proper consideration'. They also agreed, then and there, to have weekly meetings to restore communications while such major changes were in the air. However, Campbell knew this would not resolve the underlying problem. He had to sell his labour force a fundamentally new style of work. How?

Option one
| Tell them to take it or leave it? |

Option two
| Take them aside individually and talk to each one of them face to face? |

Option three
| Tell them collectively and give them a chance to air their grievances? |

It is unlikely that Campbell would take option one, although there was a time when he would have done so. Campbell has come a long way in the new world of Vulcan. Instead, he opts for a rather subtle approach, as we shall see.

*T*HEORY

Workers at Vulcan, and elsewhere, often resist change which they see as being imposed upon them. For the manager, resistance can seem like rebellion; moreover, rebellion against essentially trivial alteration. Generally, the more marked the reaction, the greater the threat perceived by the workforce – regardless of whether the change is, or is not, a true threat. It is the duty of managers to anticipate such reactions during times of change and to alleviate them. No one will react to a set pattern, but on Campbell's assembly lines the dominating emotions for the workers are likely to be:

■ **Discomfort** at the prospect of abandoning habits. Unskilled and skilled manual workers alike are to some extent creatures of habit. Their performance depends on well-learned routines and assimilating new ones means extra work.

■ **Self-interest** Who will gain from the new pecking order, arising from introducing new skills? The three supervisors are skilled in overseeing a complex assembly process. Will they still have their edge when they become overseers of a simpler, but faster-moving, process?

■ **Insecurity** Vulcan is obviously going for quick profit: which, to people who actually make the products, means job losses.

■ **Lack of trust** They know that there are other changes in the pipeline, but these have have not been aired at their level; the excitement has not been shared, and so they are suspicious.

There were four different tactics which Campbell could use to overcome resistance; on this occasion, he used them all, and cleverly and patiently outmanoeuvred the doubters.

■ **Negotiation** When resistance stems from self-interest, point out the advantages of the new development, but say that you cannot guarantee the benefits unless you have the commitment. In this instance, Campbell won over Riley by demonstrating how much easier it would be for the workforce to earn its standard productivity-related bonus once the new system was working.

■ **Education** Campbell, realizing that there was a mountain of ignorance beneath him, knew he had to spend time explaining the developments, initially to his supervisors and then, in a meeting convened by them, to the wider audience of the workforce.

■ **Involvement** Campbell allocated (for him) an exceptionally large number of man-hours for the supervisors, to re-design the production lines so that part-finished goods could be moved quickly to the new workstations. He would usually have done this himself, with his A-team as helpers, in half the time.

■ **Force and support** This means imposing the change whether the workforce likes it or not, but sustaining it by extra input of supportive management after implementation. The approach works best in situations where imagined fear of change is greater than that which is actuallly justified.

C HECKLIST

Checklist for implementing wholesale change.

■ **Prepare the ground**, minimize surprise.

■ **Tell the workforce about change**, and start by saying that there are to be exciting developments – THEN emphasize that no change, however major, is total and then list what will not be changing. Keep it factual. (Vulcan, for instance, was still going to make some of its products.)

■ **Define the changes in terms of jobs.** "The supervisors will have to take much more control of goods coming in because they will cost so much more than the simple bits used previously." Don't generalize – it makes people think that you are leaving yourself room to manoeuvre.

■ **Use the line management structure**. You are unlikely to appreciate the full details of the job at assembly-line level; so MOTIVATE THE SUPERVISORS instead. They, in turn, will motivate the workforce.

■ **Anticipate** how workers will react. Rehearse answers to likely questions.

■ **Monitor progress** and be prepared to change your tactics and schedule.

E XERCISE

Think of a change which has been imposed on you at work.

How was it achieved by the manager(s) responsible?

Rate the managers on a scale of one to ten for

- negotiating
- educating
- involving
- force and support

Where they score less than seven, think of ways in which, in their place, you could have scored seven or higher.

STRESS

> "If work were such a good thing, then the rich would have hogged it long ago."
> Mark Twain
>
> "They have, Mr Twain."
> Charles Handy

Dear Stuart,

This is to inform you that I shall be leaving Vulcan in three months' time to resume my academic career. I have always wanted the opportunity to complete my degree and now the chance has presented itself. My girlfriend, Jessica, has just been promoted and because of this our finances can just about stand the move. We both feel that if I don't do it now, I never will.

Thank you for a fascinating introduction to the world of business. I have enjoyed my time at Vulcan and feel that the experience will stand me in good stead for the future. I will never forget the kindness and consideration you showed me throughout my stay here.

I wish you and Monica all the best for the future.

Yours,

Matthew

P.S. I trust that you will be able to give me a favourable reference.

Stuart put the letter down and sighed with relief. He knew that this was the best possible outcome for all concerned but he still genuinely believed that Matthew had the potential to become a first-class manager.

Perhaps it had been unrealistic to have expected Matthew to have handled so much pressure in his first major job. Suddenly, Stuart felt drained. The last 12 months had been tough. In Stuart's mind, there was no doubt that it was the stress of uncertainty over his position which had finally made Matthew resign: slow-burning pressure which had been brought to a head by Betty's outburst in *case study 29* and the fact that Stuart did not immediately accept her resignation. This had finally brought the message home to Matthew: rightly or wrongly, Betty's dynamism was of more value to Stuart than Matthew's ideas and training.

If Stuart had seen off Matthew, how were the others handling the strain?

"I've got to alleviate the stress," he said to Helen. "I'm worried that Matthew's opting out may put similar ideas into the others' minds."

Without some tension, properly chanelled, managers rarely achieve excellence. There were times when Stuart positively enjoyed the pressure; but not now. He would leave for home early this weekend.

THEORY

Stress has two different forms:

1 Distress The everyday, grinding mixture of pressure and fear: 'Is my job secure, will my rival be promoted before me? How can I meet these impossible deadlines?'

2 Eustress The prefix '*eu-*' comes from ancient Greek and means 'good', as in 'euphoria'. Eustress is positive extra energy, as when you feel 'psyched up'.

The key to stress management is to reduce distress and encourage eustress. Clinical studies have established beyond much doubt which are the responses to stress most likely to reduce the first and give the second a sporting chance:

1 Managers who don't get emotional about pressure generally make the best showing. *This is how Stuart usually responds under pressure.*
2 Next come those managers who get keyed up, but who are able to focus their thoughts and energies positively. *Alan operates in this way.*
3 Third are those who get annoyed, irritated or angry and express their feelings openly. *Betty is a typical example.*
4 Rather more vulnerable to distress are those who hide their feelings. *Campbell and Helen come into this category.*
5 Most vulnerable of all are those who lose their cool, and their control. *This is how Matthew sometimes reacts.*

Too many managers don't try to reduce the stress in their life. It is as if they are programmed to auto-destruct. They often suffer from a guilt complex about not working hard enough and are too concerned about trying to please their superiors or their families.

Why, when we are aware that we are causing ourselves unnecessary stress, are we incapable of doing anything about it? The psychologist Albert Ellis offers some answers.

He describes four belief systems which he believes cause "nine-tenths of all human suffering". They are:

Belief system one That there is an overall purpose for the universe of which we are a part. This order extends to individual problems: for example, Betty believes absolutely that 'It will be alright on the night', as if there were somebody out there who had laid down the rule, just for her.

Unfortunately, it is not 'always alright on the night' for Betty, or for anyone else. When people who operate within this belief system experience failure and frustration, they suddenly feel the bottom dropping out of their world. Whatever it is 'out there' has suddenly become capricious, treacherous. The resulting distress is intense and can only be overcome by 'forgetting' the incident and 'hoping for better luck next time'. Next time, however, the feeling of being let down will probably be worse.

Belief system two That organizations and hierarchies can solve human problems; that because people have superior status then they must in themselves be superior. People who live by this system say things like: "The boss knows best." They also believe that 'the company owes me a living', or 'because I was good once, they will pay me for ever'. Duncan Johnson's way of managing the company had led many of his employees into this belief system.

The rationalisations and redundancies that Stuart imposed caused them particular distress.

Belief system three That other people should conform to our own standards or beliefs. This particular belief is at the root of many of the stress problems of Stuart and his team. Because they are so vitally concerned with survival, they work all hours available. Stuart alone is doing 60 hours a week. Because he is on the job almost all his waking hours, he would be forced to plan his tasks into the time available, rather than just throw time at the tasks. Also, people around him were beginning to take his time for granted, and to impose on him. Only last week a member of staff had knocked on his office door and given him the keys: "Would you mind locking up for me, Mr Blyth? I have to go now."

Stuart is also beginning to feel badly about staff who, although dedicated, are not working the same hours. Recently, one of his younger managers had remarked that he would be leaving at 18.30 – so that he could be at home for his newly-born son's bath. Stuart said tetchily: "OK, go home and leave the job to the people who can take the pace."

Belief system four That we must behave in a certain way to be a 'good person'. The belief is probably set by our parents who 'expect' certain things from us – success at school, grand-children, and so on. In childhood and youth, we feel that our parents will reject us if we fail to reach these targets. As we grow into adulthood, we feel 'bad' about ourselves if we 'fail'. This adds an extra layer of pressure to the existing stress and makes us perform even worse than we otherwise might.

E<small>XERCISE</small>

Recognize the immediate physical signs of stress:
- Dry mouth.
- Sweating.
- Prickly heat in arms or legs.
- Confused thought patterns and speech.
- A need to empty the bowels.

All these are symptomatic of the body gearing up for 'fight or flight'. Fighting or running away were essential to survival when humans were primitive hunters in the jungle. In the modern office jungle, such reactions are inappropriate; they involve a dramatic increase in the heart rate.

How often do you suffer from one or all of these symptoms?

The secondary signs of stress are ways of nullifying – or seem to be ways of nullifying – the problem.
- Alcohol.
- Over-eating.
- Inappropriate display of emotion.

The tertiary responses are hidden within us – for a while, at least. The internal organs react to the long-term primary and secondary manifestations of stress, with consequences such as heart disease and cancer. By then it is often too late.

Now look again at the four belief systems discussed above. Which of them do you subscribe to? It could be one or more. Imagine abandoning the belief. Now visualize a stressful situation. How do you react?

ALL CHANGE

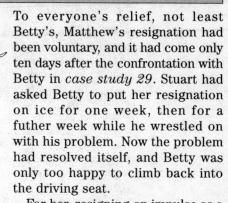

To everyone's relief, not least Betty's, Matthew's resignation had been voluntary, and it had come only ten days after the confrontation with Betty in *case study 29*. Stuart had asked Betty to put her resignation on ice for one week, then for a futher week while he wrestled on with his problem. Now the problem had resolved itself, and Betty was only too happy to climb back into the driving seat.

For her, resigning on impulse as a matter of principle had been an enjoyable experience. Without dependents, and with plenty of contacts in the industry, she had been confident of finding another post, probably in a more secure company than Vulcan. Now she was on her way to Campbell's office.

"Got a minute?"

Campbell, who knew this meant at least an hour of discussion, smiled and allowed Betty to pour out her concerns.

"The new product, can you make it?"

"Kid, we can make anything. You tell us, we make it." Campbell knew how to wind Betty up.

"Campbell, I'm serious. Can you make it?"

"Come on Betty, you know the answer as well as I do. We can make the electronic notebook in theory; in fact, we can do it in practice – you've seen the prototype. But on the other hand, it's put together from different components and that gives me worries. Everyone feels the same, especially the purchasing department. They've got to work with completely new suppliers on the other side of the world who don't speak their language. That makes them worried. I can't wave a magic wand and promise them trouble-free production."

Betty was planning a deeply discounted opening offer of the electronic notebook. In order for Vulcan to make any money on this, the product would have to be sold direct to retailers, cutting out the wholesaler's margin. She knew that the offer would fall flat on its face if Vulcan could not service the retailers with the volume required. Bulk delivery of parts from the Far East had yet to begin. Until all the bits were in the store rooms, the outcome was unknown. Her major retail accounts would expect assurance of trouble-free supply in return for giving the product major window displays. Betty had to make a judgement on how ambitious a launch she should plan, but without proper information.

What should Betty do?

Option one

Push ahead, hoping that things will work out OK?

Option two

Allow for the possibility of poor supply and design a lower-key launch that was not so dependent on readily available, large volumes of stock?

Whichever option she chose, Betty realized that Stuart and the rest of the board would expect from her a rational assurance of the relationship between risk and reward. She wanted to show them that, when the occasion demanded it, she was not solely a creature of impulse. How could she analyse all the factors, and put them across in a simple but convincing way?

THEORY

A commercial venture can be likened to a cube. Any change in any one of the six faces brings into play the 'unknown'.

⚀ The product itself

⚁ The way in which the product is sold – retail, wholesale, or direct mail

⚂ The suppliers that provide the raw materials

⚃ The process by which the product is made or assembled

⚄ The customers to whom the product is sold

⚅ The way the manufacture is financed, and how the the customers pay

As a general rule of thumb, the risk of changing three or more of the six faces at one time is usually too great for an organization to accept. Betty is proposing to change three out of six factors: only customers, distribution and finance remain as they were. The assembly process is different; the product is different; and Betty was planning to sell it direct to retail chains rather than through Vulcan's existing wholesalers. Of course, the six factors carry different levels of risk, but the cube analogy has the great advantage of giving one's thoughts an initial clarity and focus.

Betty saw that the level of risk was unacceptable and began trying to work out how to reduce it. The only face on which she could work was the method of sale, but the more she looked at this, the more she realized that she would have to revise her scheme for a sensationally low opening retail offer. Her team did not have the experience of selling direct to retail chains.

Stuart agreed – reluctantly – because he, like Betty, wanted to take the market by storm. They decided they would sell the new product in the traditional way via wholesalers for the first six months, which would give Betty time to improve her existing relationships with the major retail outlets. Perhaps they would be able to run a price-slashed offer in January or February of the product's second year.

*E*XERCISE

■ Brainstorm new products, processes or services for your organization.

■ Think of each new item in terms of profit to the company and devise an order of preference.

■ Look at the same list in terms of risk – how near is it to what we know?

■ Consider the trade-off – high risk/high profit, low risk/low profit.

ASSESSING
THE RISK OF CHANGE

> There is nothing more difficult to take in hand, more perilous to conduct, or more uncertain in its success, than to take the lead in the introduction of a new order of things, because the innovator has for enemies all those who have done well under the old conditions, and lukewarm defenders in those who may do well under the new
>
> Machiavelli (1446-1507), *The Prince*

Alan had known that there would be only one winner when Matthew took on Betty and he suspected that Betty's resignation had been a ploy to test her own position at Vulcan. As Alan saw it, she had had nothing to lose. If Stuart had valued her above Matthew, he would have persuaded her to stay; and Matthew would have been fired. If she was wrong, and Matthew was indeed the 'golden boy', she needed to go anyway. Her resignation had forced the issue and Alan now wished that he could sort out his own position at Vulcan as quickly and decisively.

For, since he had overcome his crisis in *case study 2*, the game had changed again, this time perhaps more radically.

Betty's victory, and the pinning of so much hope on the new product, meant in effect that Vulcan was to become much more of an ideas- and marketing-led company than before.

Alan, at this juncture, was not concerned with whether he would fit into this new style of organization. He had proved to himself, in overcoming the Matthew threat, and by the fact that Stuart now found him indispensable, that he could easily survive Vulcan's internal challenges.

He was much more concerned whether Vulcan itself could live up to its new role; whether the organization, and the existing team, were capable of being winners. If not, his best option would be early retirement.

> Alan reckoned that there was a real danger that Vulcan's existing workforce and managers at all levels would find themselves deeply uncomfortable with the new product and the new way of working; that there would be redundancies and voluntary departures among the workforce; that Campbell, although currently committed, would probably resign if life became too hellish in the assembly area. If that happened, Betty would be unable to supply the customers adequately, and quickly lose patience. If these two key people did not actually abandon the fight, they might easily threaten to do so, putting Stuart under appalling pressure.
>
> Alan wanted to know whether, under these circumstances, Stuart would:
>
> ■ **Give up** – finally disillusioned with the poor quality of his team. For, as Alan saw it, the whole team was third-rate compared with Stuart. Or would Stuart
>
> ■ **Carry on** – re-motivating the team or, if necessary, hiring replacements?
>
> *What do you think?* Alan's verdict was that Stuart would carry on despite all the difficulties, and he was right. *But how did he reach this view?*

THEORY

This is, of course, a highly speculative area. You therefore need to anchor your thoughts in something as concrete as possible. Probably the easiest way is to find historical models or analogies for the people you are trying to judge.

Alan naturally settled on Duncan Johnson, his old boss, as the most obvious model. He had always seen Johnson as an essentially feudal person. He would rather have closed the whole company than make major redundancies and thus lose the respect of 'his' people.

The analogy – the comparison of Stuart with this historical model – was instructive. By comparison, Stuart was much less idealistic; more like Patton, the American tank commander in the Second World War. Patton treated his forces like a private army with an overriding mission to reach Berlin first. He would have been perfectly comfortable, Alan surmised, in taking on a new design of tank, provided it was reasonably likely to get him to Berlin first.

Stuart, likewise, would embrace new ideas much more readily than Duncan Johnson; he did not worry if they offended people, and if they failed, he simply found new ones.

Alan now recalled the way Stuart had shrugged off the failure of the Thompson bid and simply started afresh. Could Duncan Johnson have weathered that farrago in the same way? Alan had seen him struggle with some lesser disappointments: they had made him too depressed to work properly for several weeks.

Stuart simply was not a man to get bogged

down by failure or misfortune, which was why he had such a convincing record for reviving sick companies.

Historical analogies, such as the ones described above, can be used to help you form judgements of complex situations in several different ways.

First, as above, you can compare an individual to another individual in history.

Secondly, you can compare the individual with his behaviour in his own past.

Finally, you liken a whole organization to an historic individual or institution.

*E*XERCISE

Reflect on your own company or organization and its chief executive. Think up historical analogies for their current circumstances. Then imagine a major change that might overtake the organization. Use the analogy to rate the chief executive's likelihood of survival: has he or she a better than 50 per cent chance, or worse?

PONDERING THE FUTURE

> "Have we permanent friends?"
> "Madam, we have no permanent friends or permanent enemies, only permanent interests."
> Prime Minister Gladstone in conversation with Queen Victoria

Helen was working with Matthew on his leaving formalities when he said: "I was convinced you wouldn't make the grade when I first came here. I was wrong. You've changed."

"No I haven't," replied Helen. "It's the company which has changed, not me."

They let the subject drop for a while, until Matthew said: "Yes, I suppose you're right. Do you know, I'm beginning to have doubts about leaving here myself."

"I know what you mean, Matthew. I'm really enjoying myself here – it's become exciting, a real challenge. You weren't here when Duncan Johnson was in charge. It was completely different."

She went on: "The trouble was, he was the only boss I'd ever worked for. I didn't realize there was another way to run a business. Under Stuart, Vulcan has become a different animal."

Matthew nodded: "Yes, the change has brought out your best qualities. People around here never believed that a personnel director could play a significant part in shaping the company's future. Everyone is saying that it was the way you brought off the innovation search that has given Vulcan its new lease of life."

Helen allowed herself to savour the moment. It was, she knew, a real achievement to make personnel, by tradition an uncreative service department, contribute measurably to the growth of a business.

At the same time, she saw that despite this achievement, her position at Vulcan was not necessarily more secure than it had been when Stuart had complained, soon after his arrival (*case study 4*) about her rambling memos.

The following Friday, at Matthew's leaving party, she had an amusing interlude with Matthew, swapping joke newspaper headlines about Vulcan's future.

> "Wilson's massive bid for Stock Exchange star Vulcan Computers is now subject to a counter bid by I.B.M.",

suggested Matthew.

> "Demand for Vulcan's products has dropped dramatically – massive redundancies imminent,"

countered Helen.

> "Stuart Blyth, head of Vulcan Computers, has just won the take-over for I.B.M.",

was Matthew's next offering. "Or", he said, "how about:

> "Leveraged buy-out specialist Matthew Davies, who began his career at Vulcan Computers, today realized his life-long ambition of taking over the company. The firm of which he is a partner now has a major stake."

The words "buy-out" brought Helen up short – although she betrayed nothing to Matthew.

Her instincts told her that changes were by no means over for Vulcan. It seemed more important than ever to work out where the changes left her and what her next move should be to keep up the momentum of her career.

> **How would you set about analysing Helen's priorities?**

Remember, her core job is to ensure that Vulcan has the right personnel, correctly trained and qualified, to operate Vulcan's business.

■ People expect personnel officers to come to the rescue as soon as needs arise. No one would thank her for coming up with new staff, however good, after they were needed.

■ Should she be putting proposals to Stuart about a replacement for Matthew? Should she be persuading Campbell to send his workforce on retraining courses? Should she, now that the company was to be much more marketing-oriented, research the best young names as potential recruits to an expanded marketing department?

Helen reached her conclusions by systematically analysing the Vulcan operation under a sequence of headings which she called the 'five spinning plates of the aware manager'.

*T*HEORY

The manager who wants to keep ahead of the game, rather than wonder what happened when it is too late, can do worse than imagine him- or herself as a circus artist trying to keep five plates constantly spinning. They are:

> *1* The purpose – the organization's mission statement.
>
> *2* The team.
>
> *3* Rewards and motivation.
>
> *4* The organization and its structures.
>
> *5* Goodwill – formal and informal support that the organization enjoys in the market and in the community.

So integral and inter-related are these five themes to the running of an organization that allowing one to fall has a knock-on effect on the others, eventually making them all collapse.

Helen's immediate perception was that Vulcan's new mission, essentially the change from basic manufacturing to assembly, meant that Vulcan might lose goodwill in its local recruiting grounds, resulting in difficulties with the manning of the plant.

She also saw the company's existing organization and structure as essentially defined by its top management team. Under Duncan Johnson, the top managers fulfilled the needs and wishes of a one-man expert and autocrat. Campbell had had to consult Johnson about every minor production change. By complete contrast, Stuart was not a computer person, but a skilled manager who understood money. His organisation had – painfully – become one of delegation and trust. Campbell and his research and development team were now the source of new technologies, and Betty of new marketing ideas. It was even clearer now to Helen why Matthew had had to go – he was not a team player and never would be. Under Johnson he might have developed, but his individuality meant that he would never be trusted or trust others. He needed to be closely controlled and that was not Stuart's style.

This analysis of the organization led Helen straight to the **team**. If the numbers working in Cambell's production unit were going to fall, the balance of the company would shift from manufacturing to marketing, and, she suspected, to purchasing.

Perhaps Matthew's successor should be a purchasing director with a knowledge of far-eastern languages? Helen saw herself having a long conversation with Stuart about this. The organization, although building firmly on the foundations Stuart had laid, would have to change again. Next, she came to **rewards**. Helen's rewards during the last year had been immense – as Matthew had pointed out, she had grown. Money was not an issue with her – except in that she hoped, during the next year, she might have some time to spend some of what she earned. She suspected that Alan, and probably Stuart, felt the same. And what about Betty? She too had grown, and probably found satisfaction in this. She probably wanted more money; the new product offered the promise of that.

Finally, there was Campbell. He would lose much of his power in the shake-up. He loved his empire and was none too happy with the Taskens of this world – they made him feel old. Campbell's rewards might be endangered by the current changes. Something else to discuss with Stuart. Out of Helen's systematic analysis of how to keep the plates spinning came, therefore, two urgent priorities for Helen. First, to do some private research into how and where she might recruit a purchasing executive with expertise in the Far East. She wanted to be ready with suggestions before Stuart or anyone else raised the question.

Secondly, she had to think up ways of strengthening Campbell's position so that balance in the top management team could be maintained.

*E*XERCISE

Managers tend to be experts at keeping just one or two of these five plates spinning: they think solely in terms of team spirit, for example, or of motivation and rewards.

● Which plate or plates do you tend to concentrate on?

● Put those plates aside and think about the others. In a stable situation, thinking about one or two plates is probably OK. But not in times of change.

Imagine that a shake-up is to happen in your organization next year. Analyse, as Helen did, what moves you can make ahead of time to keep all the plates spinning during, and beyond, the period of change.

THE BOMBSHELL

> I have a dream...
> Martin Luther King

Stuart decided that the time was ripe to make his announcement.

Betty had just completed some test marketing on the new product. A few expensively produced prototypes had been loaned to colleges and universities across the country. The results, now coming in, were much more revealing than the consumer trials conducted just after the notebook had been originally designed.

Several colleges had telephoned Vulcan to ask where they could buy the notebook, and the students who had tried the prototypes were saying that they would not work without them.

Betty had just started presenting the product to wholesalers, and the first orders were for large numbers. So large, in fact, that Betty was in Campbell's office every day challenging him to increase production. It was no longer "Can you..." but "How quickly can you..." Campbell's shell-shocked purchasers found themselves scouring Taiwan for such large numbers of parts that they could re-negotiate their prices by as much as 20 per cent lower than those paid on the first buying round. This meant that the manufacturing unit cost of the notebook would drop well below the original estimate; the profit would rise in turn.

Alan, working alongside Stuart, had used these figures to write an updated cash flow projection for Vulcan. (It was just as professionally prepared and presented as any of Matthews' had been, and, Stuart mused, the work had been completed much more quickly than it would have been by Matthew, who had always needed to show off his professionalism by combing through the implications of every side issue.)

The cash plan showed, on the most conservative estimate, that Vulcan would not only go cash-positive within 60 days of the launch (this for the first time in three years) but that its profits at the end of the coming financial year would be beyond everyone's dreams.

Stuart coolly unveiled this forecast, and then said:

"I have a proposal. I've checked it out with the bank and they're enthusiastic. The figures stack up, but there's still plenty of work to do on it. First, though, I need your reactions."

"What is it?" Betty could hardly get the words out.

"*A management buy-out.*"

"You mean we buy the company from the existing shareholders?" Alan gasped. His initial reaction was mixed. It was a great idea, but what about his age? (Then he heard another voice inside his head saying "There you go again, worrying about trivia...")

Campbell could not take it in. He and his wife had been expecting the worst for the last 12 months, and had been closer than ever to going into the antiques business full-time. Now this. He was not sure how it could be done. Would it mean having to raise tens of thousands? What security would he have to provide?

Helen was the least surprised. "In for a penny, in for a pound", she smiled to herself, neatly summarizing Stuart's motives for the scheme. Making the directors more or less solely responsible for their own well-being, and thereby the company's, was the logical conclusion of his entire management philosophy. He had probably been nurturing the idea since the day he arrived, certainly since the famous board meeting (*case study 19*) when he prophesied that Vulcan would rise from the ashes. All he had lacked was the opportunity.

Betty was already visualizing herself behind the wheel of a Porsche; in fact, she was internally debating whether or not to go for a white bucksin seat-trim.

> **Do you think that Stuart was right in supposing that his team was ready to take on this challenge?**

In order to reach your conclusions, you can assume that Vulcan's capital structure was ideal for a buy-out. The share price was depressed and the existing investors mainly institutional, keen to see their stake gain in value. Given that the prospects, the financial nuts and bolts and the timing were perfect for a leveraged buy-out, how do you assess the all-important, and much more variable factor of the individuals concerned?

> *How would they face up to the rigours of taking on personal debt in order to own a significant stake in their company?*
>
> ■ Is Alan too old?
>
> ■ Is Campbell too conservative?
>
> ■ Is Betty too impetuous?
>
> ■ Is Helen a leader yet?
>
> ■ Should they replace Matthew?
>
> ■ Does Stuart have a well-balanced enough team with the necessary skills?

There is no cut-and-dried answer to these questions. Stuart was sure, after pondering what the individual reactions were likely to be, that the team would eventually come round to the idea. He was now asking for confirmation that his hunch was correct.

Had Campbell, for instance, already made up his mind to leave Vulcan? Would Alan, decide that the chance had come too late for him? No doubt Betty would jump at the oppor-tunity; Helen, by contrast, might come under pressure at home to settle for the easy life.

How would you go about trying to predict the individual reactions?

*T*HEORY

It is possible to assess in a surprisingly precise way how different individuals will respond to major change.

Most people can, of course, tolerate mild change: change which does not deny their **personal identity**, their **values and beliefs**, their **skills**, their **behaviour** or their **environment**. Most individuals have a special concern with one or two of these key factors.

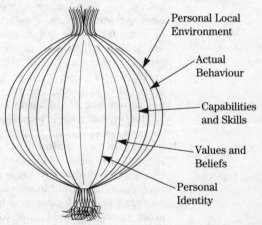

Personal Local Environment

Actual Behaviour

Capabilities and Skills

Values and Beliefs

Personal Identity

Stuart is principally concerned with his identity as chief executive. The buy-out would not affect this identity, in fact owning part of the company would enhance it. Nor would the buy-out compromise his dominant values and beliefs, namely the work ethic (the harder you try, the more you succeed). It is not surprising that on both these counts, Stuart is very keen indeed on the buy-out idea.

As Stuart talked in greater detail about how the buy-out would work, Campbell began instinctively to assess the change in terms of his skills. He saw that instead of being an unchalleneged expert in his field, from now on he would have to talk on more equal terms to his fellow-shareholders in the boardroom.

Alan worried about whether his behaviour would be in keeping with the new-style Vulcan. He did not feel old, but he thought others saw him as an old-timer and that, he felt, might undermine his standing in a new, more demanding environment.

Helen still saw herself, perhaps wrongly, as a helper, not as a leader: her values and beliefs were essentially moral – she was more interested in caring for people and creating a better working life for individuals than in acquiring wealth and power. Owning a slice of Vulcan seemed 'a bit much' to her; 'not really me'. But if a buy-out meant that she would be better able to realize her values, she could hardly turn it down.

The buy-out fitted Betty like a glove because she saw herself as an entrepreneur and owning a stake in the company would confirm this identity at a stroke. Perhaps even more significantly, the possibility of becoming seriously rich meant that she could improve her environment. As Stuart spoke she was wondering whether the other directors would agree to spending money on flash new offices and company cars. "Campbell, Alan and Helen are such puritans", she said to herself, "but Stuart likes fast cars and maybe I can convince him that sharing an executive jet with another local company might not be as extravagant as all that…"

Richard Bandler, the consultant psychiatrist who formulated this theory of:

- identity
- beliefs

- skills
- behaviour
- environment

as key factors in response to change, devised a neat method of quickly judging which of the five concern an individual most. You ask them to say:

> ### *We cannot do that here*
>
> Different emphasis on a different word in this sentence gives tell-tale clues about the individual's motivation:
>
> Emphasis on WE means the individual is especially concerned with his or her **identity**.
>
> Emphasis on CANNOT suggests that the individual thinks **beliefs** are especially important.
>
> Emphasis on DO means the individual's hang-up is **skills**.
>
> Emphasis on THAT indicates that individual worries about **behaviour**.
>
> Emphasis on HERE reveals an individual who attaches importance to **environment**.

*E*XERCISE

> How would different colleagues of yours deliver the sentence 'We cannot do that here'? Does it reveal their primary motivation(s)?

TRANSITION

> There used to be a me, but I had it surgically removed
>
> Peter Sellers

The four directors were in varying degrees of turmoil after the board meeting (*case study 35*) at which Stuart had proposed a management buy-out. Betty had decided instantly to go ahead, and felt only excitement. Helen, after agonizing over the deal for several nights with her husband, had decided in favour of the buy-out, too. But Alan and Campbell had had a shock.

To them, after years of working towards stable finances and safe retirement, the prospect of taking out substantial loans, secured against their homes, was frightening. They also thought that if they did not support the buy-out they would, in effect, lose their places in the team and that Stuart would recruit younger and more entrepreneurial managers to replace them. They were worried, too, about whether their skills and behaviour would stand up to the new, harsh environment that private ownership would create. The more they thought about the proposal, the more it seemed like a potentially fatal body-blow.

They were in such turmoil that they felt unable to act; certainly unable to make decisions. The fact that Vulcan was now in an excellent position financially, that it was on the brink of making enormous profits from the new product, and that the company debt arising from the buy-out could be radically reduced by selling their defence products line to the Japanese made little difference to them. The risks were still there, staring them in the face.

There were four weeks before the board would meet again to vote on the move.

If you were a close colleague of Alan's or Campbell's, how would you counsel them? There are various obvious options:

■ Walk away from the problem until they calm down?

■ Seek assurances from Stuart about their futures should they join the buy-out?

■ Analayse their financial positions and the prospects for Vulcan with the help of an independent expert?

Answer   None of these options really meets the problem, which is essentially psychological. Alan and Campbell need to understand the various transitional stages through which they are bound to go when recovering from shock, and to organize their energies accordingly.

T HEORY

The Process of Change

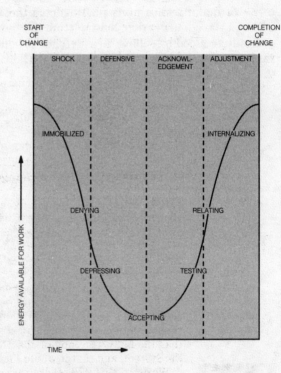

The bigger the change, the more it saps the individual's energy. The better the individual's attitude, the quicker he or she will recover.

In the initial state of emotional shock induced by change, people are, to a greater or lesser extent, immobilized. Next, they become defensive, trying to minimize the problem, but becoming increasingly depressed. As the graph bottoms out, the individual starts to accept the full implications of change in a despairing, but realistic way. The next, more positive, phase is testing and acknowledging the implications of the change, and relating these to wider issues. Helen did just this when she rang her lawyer to ask if the family savings could be put in the children's names so that at least some of the family assets would be immune from Vulcan-related risk.

The final stage is when you make the change your own – when you embrace it, for better or worse, and 'internalize it'.

A positive approach to change

Shocks will always be shocking, and change will always mean upheaval. But if people could be aware during times of change that some kind of status quo will inevitably reassert itself in their lives, they would come through the upheaval much happier people.

Alan and Campbell needed someone to tell them that the stages through which they felt themselves passing, in particular the awful sensation of being immobilized, were no more than the body's method of absorbing shock into the system, and that it would inevitably pass.

While in this phase, there was no point in trying to make decisions: they would not have the energy. Their best course would be to concentrate on routine tasks and to take some time off to visit the golf course.

They should try to hurry through the phases; but they should also beware of getting stuck in any of them.

■ If you have to deal with a colleague or friend in a state of shock, have the sensitivity, and the intelligence, to gauge whether they are passing through the stages at a healthy rate; don't hurry them through a stage just because it seems particularly unpleasant.

■ Likewise, at an organizational level, don't force the pace of change. Try to:

■ Introduce it in sensible phases. Avoid putting an entire organization into the initial stages of immobility. If possible, introduce change from the top downwards, at intervals.

■ Counsel key people about the processes they are about to unleash. Tell them to watch for signs of the upturn and to suggest to executives that they postpone major decisions about their futures until they are in the testing phase.

*E*XERCISE

Consider a recent forced change your own organization has made.

Using the model we have presented, rate how well the change was managed.

THE WAY AHEAD

> Genius is the ability to put into effect what is in your mind
>
> F. Scott Fitzgerald

Betty had half her mind on the colour of the Porsche and half her mind on the road. She did not realize that there had been an accident up ahead until she was right alongside the crumpled remains of a silver BMW. It was Stuart's.

She frantically reversed her car, turned around, and raced for the hosptial. Stuart was already dead when she arrived ten minutes later.

"And at a time when we thought everything was coming right," each stunned member of the team said automatically at the emergency board meeting next day.

"Look, I know it sounds hard-nosed", said Alan, "but life has got to go on. We've got to pull ourselves together without delay. We owe it to Stuart's memory to put this behind us; to get on with the job of making Vulcan succeed. Stuart never got bogged down by failure; nor should we."

They agreed immediately to postpone the management buy-out; and they nominated Helen to sort out Stuart's company affairs and to find out what help could be offered to his widow.

"OK," said Betty, "but how are we going to replace Stuart?"

> That is the final management problem we ask you to consider.
>
> Assuming that the four surviving directors agree that the new boss should be one of them, rather than an outsider, who would you choose? You can also assume that Stuart had left no succession plans.
>
> Our verdict is printed upside down on page

255, but resist the temptation to look until you have thought the problem through. You will have to start from scratch because, of course, no natural leader has yet emerged among the four. They are all now extremely capable managers in their own right; but one of them now has to make a leap.

Here are some pointers:

■ Betty seems outwardly confident, and she can claim to be a marketing genius; but underneath she has doubts about herself. She has heard about the Peter Principle (which says that good managers rise and rise until they get a job which is just beyond their capabilities) and suspects that her best chances of remaining a big player rest in being a star, rather than the team leader. Marketing people suffer from this perhaps more than other types of manager. Betty is already in danger of spreading herself too thin and would be the first to acknowledge that she lacks major areas of management expertise.

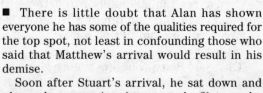

■ There is little doubt that Alan has shown everyone he has some of the qualities required for the top spot, not least in confounding those who said that Matthew's arrival would result in his demise.

Soon after Stuart's arrival, he sat down and planned a campaign (*case study 2*) to make himself indispensable to Stuart. It worked. No doubt Alan would sit down and weigh up the new situation in exactly the same, thorough way again. He is a strategist, and Vulcan's team leader needs to be exactly that.

But there are still some question marks against him. He has dwelt too much on his age and allowed it to become a personal problem, despite the fact that Stuart and the others discount it. This is symptomatic of Alan's key weakness: he can be too introspective, especially for a team leader. Also, he lacks charisma. If he took over, there would be endless committees and meetings.

■ What about Helen? She has taken everyone by surprise. The once ugly duckling has been transformed into an elegant swan, at least in managerial terms.

She has won the respect of her colleagues; there is a stream of managers making tracks to her door, seeking advice. It is freely given and she has remarkably few enemies at Vulcan. If there was a popularity poll she would come top – Betty and Campbell have upset too many people in their time, while Alan is still looked upon as being rather 'grey'.

Her understanding of management is undeniable and it is underpinned by more than a little common sense. But would she be able to stand the pressure at the top? Is she too nice? Does she have fire in her belly? On the other hand, she is good at working with people. If she got the job, she would certainly approach it in a different way to Stuart.

■ And then there is reliable Campbell – the salt of the earth – whose value has often been overlooked in the past. It was not until Stuart's arrival that Campbell began to get the respect he deserved. He is very good at his job and can stand the pressure when it counts. When the tough get going, so can Campbell. He has the right background: he understands the product, and the industry, thoroughly. He can lead from the front and push things through. He has a keen critical eye and knows his weaknesses.

His determination to improve himself – mainly with Helen's help – has held him up to ridicule from time to time, but he has persevered. He has what it takes to be a good manager, but how does he compare with Stuart?

Remember that this would be the acid test for whoever takes over. Stuart had to live in the shadow of his predecessor for a while, and it took him some time to assert himself.

We suggest that you take a highly structured look at this problem. The seeds of a solution exist in the earlier case studies, not as deliberately laid clues, but as pointers. Go back through the case studies – almost all will contribute something to the decision. Particularly important is number *20*, about the need to have balance in a team; also *21*, about motivation; and *25*, on personal development needs. Number *31*, on handling stress, is also highly relevant.

Good luck with your choice. Vulcan is going to need it.

POSTSCRIPT

STUART'S SUCCESSOR

Vulcan's bank, predictably enough, tried to force the appointment of an outside managing director of their own choice. But the days of Vulcan working for its bank, rather than the other way round, were happily at an end. Helen convincingly demonstrated, using team theory, that the outsider was merely a clone of Alan, but with less experience of the business. With very considerable cash surpluses to hand, the four surviving directors had no qualms about rejecting the bank's nominee.

At a meeting of the shareholders, it was agreed that the buy-out should be postponed for nine months, and that until then one of the major shareholders, and also Vulcan's bank manager, should be appointed temporary, non-executive directors.

It was also agreed that Alan should be the new managing director. Alan signed a two-year contract which would also make him, on his retirement, chairman and a non-executive director.

Helen was named deputy managing director, and thus became the heir apparent. If things went according to plan – she would work closely with Alan for the next two years in order to gain first-hand knowledge of Vulcan's entire financial system – Helen would become not only one of the few personnel directors to lead a company of Vulcan's size, but also one of the first women to head an electronics company.

Betty was content to remain marketing director. She not only raised a substantial loan on her house, but borrowed a large sum of money from her wealthy contacts, including her father. She was to take a major personal stake in Vulcan: if the buy-out worked, she could buy not just the Porsche, but a fleet of high-performance cars.

Apart from being lit up with enthusiasm for the buy-out and the money it might make her, Betty was delighted with the new hierarchical situation.

She saw that Helen and Alan would cover for each others' weaknesses, and that they had complementary strengths. She regarded Helen as more of a 'company person' than herself, and thus more suitable for the top job.

Which leaves Campbell. He was, for a while, resentful that Helen had become the heir to Vulcan. Campbell had a taste for power; he ran the biggest empire within the company, with more employees under his control than any of the other top managers. With the shift from straight manufacture to assembly, this power was being eroded. But now Helen proposed to Alan, and Alan suggested to Campbell, that he took on a new job within Vulcan: that of production and purchasing director.

Purchasing components had now become a key activity, and purchasing was to become a department in its own right, with a new manager appointed from outside: George Tai, a second-generation Korean immigrant who had the contacts, and the languages, to make Vulcan's purchasing truly professional, joined the company just three months after Stuart's death.

Campbell's status, and salary, were thus enhanced. He was re-motivated and reaffirmed in his more or less unassailable position.

If things worked out with George Tai, he would become purchasing director on Alan's retirement, but still report to Campbell. He was only 34, Helen mused, but had many of Stuart's qualities. 'With any luck, he'll be ready to take over the top job within ten years; then I can go back to being a personnel director – maybe even write a book of management advice in my spare time.'